and a good dinner you
my favorite restaurant
hope you have enough
to stay. I am telling
one about the
inn. thank you

LET ME KNOW WHEN
GET TIRED OF BEING
CONGRATULATED SO MUCH
FOR BEING SO AWESOME
CONGRATS ON YOUR 30s

happy to let folks coming
our condo who don't think
know about all the
you still have available. Hope
for us. Unit

so proud to have
your caliber.
many thanks
the best
to you
guys!

Sincerely

going to think that
matter at what age
too sudden.

the upcoming week
for you.
and los
instead the recent stroke. I hope hope you and your
collection family are doing
memories in are getting the proper rest
in your need to get better.

I'm always enjoyed hear

Sincer.

Passed by your
+ was thinking
the other day. I

Wishing you the

Thank you so much
hosting Brady + Pip
day. I did not
such creative fu
activities. You prob
know this but you
a little that da
I had a lot of

Clever talk about you
very large
an empire!

thank you for the exceptional
job you have done while here
at W.P. — I also want to
Thank you for taking care of
me when I was sick in Kansas
City! No one would have
done so much to help
another person.

Your future is so bright!
Enjoy your new job and
keep us in the winners circle

Congratulations

new home! I feel
work with
happy people
life of couple
special

My Darling Wife
This note is to warn
filet entered into by
friends (ha!) calendar
own children. There
you believe we've been
20 minutes maybe
the first place it
a human cannot

over my
cuts down
hauls them down
in freezing cold
single mom
all the heat in the
for your boys. And
real estate with

I feel such grat
you. You've played such a
role in all my major
in Seattle. Your incredible
being an amazing real e
Broker and being a lovely
really strikes me. I've bene
often and after my

First published by Hiccup Press
October 2022

ISBN 979-8-9870903-0-5

Cover photo by Kate Macate from Unsplash.com
Book design by Adam Robinson for Good Book Developers
The Sankofa Bird logo from The Noun Project

The Sankofa Bird, depicted reaching backwards for its egg, is an ancient
symbol of the Akan tribe in Ghana. It means to "go back to the past and
bring forward that which is useful." Connecting our past with the present
allows us to understand what impacts our future. We can't change what's
already happened, but we can choose how to move forward. And we honor
those who've gone before us and shown through their experiences—their
mistakes and their wisdom alike—how we can endure and thrive.

Please visit CarriePierceNotes.com

Special Thanks

Special thanks to Diana, Mike, Rachel, Adam, Laura,
Steve, Robert, Bunny, Colette, Brady and Piper for your
infinite wisdom and encouragement along the way.

Handwritten NOTES

Learn How a Small, Powerful Act Can Enrich Your Life

CARRIE PIERCE

Contents

To my dad, who fired me up with motivational sayings like "only lazy people write books."

Handwritten Notes

Learn How a Small, Powerful Act Can Enrich Your Life

"One is only happy in proportion as he makes others feel happy …"

—MS Hershey

Introduction

This book is an invitation to reexamine old ways of think-ing, to take the best of the good ole days and intermingle it into your world today. It invites you to revisit a time before distractions replaced focused thought and when human interactions were more intimate and genuine. In particular, handwritten notes were frequently used to communicate long before technology and e-communications became the norm. If you read the book closely enough you might convince yourself that this practice of writing notes by hand and sending them out into the world can do more than simply express thoughts, it can actually fill your life with greater joy and abundance. I've seen it work for me and it can work for you too.

I know, you probably think that sounds ridiculous. As I read it over, it sounds a little crazy to me too. But it's true and if you hear me out in the pages of this book you'll see how I've reaped the benefits enough that it has become a ritual in my life. When I want to deepen my relationships and "fill my own cup" so to speak, I write hand-written notes. I write them to everyone, I write them to people I love and to total strangers. I write them to friends, family, and business connections. I even once wrote a note to my brother from his feral cat. My handwriting is only so-so. My grammar and spelling are not always on point. I often don't have the right paper or pen at hand. But I don't care. I keep at it because I have seen the difference writing a heart-felt, sincere note and sending it off into the world can make for both the sender and the receiver. It has become my habit, my way-of-life—my ministry.

I tell everyone who will listen, *this stuff is magic*. In a disconnected and disengaged world full of loneliness and empty communication, writing personal notes can deepen connections and create meaningful community.

Writing hand-written notes has become a lost art of sorts. How many people do you know write them? How often do you receive them? If you're one of the lucky few who receive notes, how does that connect you with the writer of the note? The more I investigated it's impact, the more I realized I had to look into this whole note writing business a little deeper. Was I crazy? Or too old-fashioned? Or was there really something behind what I was doing? What precisely about writing notes by hand made their power so extraordinary?

It turns out there's real science behind this note writing business. In these pages, I'll lay out the neuroscience that proves that there is true power in handwritten words as opposed to the digital or typed word. You'll hear psychological studies that explain why the process of writing and receiving handwritten notes is so important to our well-being, especially in this age of ever-advancing technology. You'll read famous notes of powerful and successful people that break down just what exactly these people intuitively understood about humanity and note writing that made them so powerful and successful in the first place. I'll share with you my own personal stories of seeing all this science, psychology, and historical data play out in my own life and in the lives of others around me. The proof is in the pudding.

As I put this book together—researching, studying, and compiling data—I realized that I had not hit on something big. I had hit on something small that had big and compelling ramifications behind it. Something so small, in fact, that every person could do it every day. This is where I will tell you about my second passion after note writing: the philosophy of Dale Carnegie.

Dale Carnegie was the author of *How to Win Friends and Influence People,* the 1936 bestseller that is still in print today. He has sold over thirty million copies, making it one of the bestselling books of all time. As I went deeper and deeper into my research on handwritten notes, I began to see the parallels between Carnegie's ideas about how to find success and happiness and what I was learning about writing notes. Carnegie had big ideas. Timeless ideas that are just as viable today as they will be 100 years into the future. With his philosophy we can find small ways to act on his ideas every day, to make them habit and to manifest them in our life. By writing handwritten notes, we can change the way we are in the world.

My hope for you is that you experience this same power in your life. In these pages, you'll be taken through a step-by-step process showing you how to write the engaging type of notes that deepen personal connections and build friendships, which Carnegie (and science) tells us are one of the only routes to true happiness. You will see multiple examples of how to write notes that deeply influence the only route to lasting and remarkably effortless business success. By integrating Carnegie's insights into your note writing, you'll understand the impact of this small act. By the time you're done reading these pages, you will know exactly how to do what I did and why it works.

It will be so clear that my biggest fear in writing this book is that in taking apart and analyzing why notes "work," the people to whom I send my own notes will think the notes I've written then were all part of some habit, that they hold some degree of insincerity. This is not the case and as you read on, you'll see that sincerity and authenticity in thought and expression is absolutely key to impactful note writing. To those people I've written notes to in the past, and there are many of you, I just want to say you are as special as the note you receive. In fact, due to my not really being all that great of a writer, you're most likely much more special than my notes could ever capture. One of the biggest lessons of note writing is that the "how" and the "why" of handwritten notes needs to be put away when you set out to write a good one.

Here's the real key to the magic: to write my notes, I sit down and think about another human being for a long time. I put away distractions like phone and internet and I spend focused time thinking about what makes the other person special, what makes them unique, and what I appreciate about them. Starting from this genuine place of curiosity with an honest desire to connect to and elevate another person is the only way to write a worthwhile note. If you're out to manipulate or get what you want, this book is not for you. If you're in this for your own benefit, then you should stop reading right now because note writing will be a waste of your time. You need to be sincere in your desire to deeply connect with other humans. At risk of bringing the cheese factor to the book, notes are about filling your own soul and others'. You must want nothing else in return. In other words, when I write a note, I take all this science and reason and throw it out the window. I go back to the intuition and human feeling that made me want to write notes in the first place.

These notes are dear to me. My life story can be told through the notes I've written and received. Handwritten notes helped me through an anxious childhood with two loving, hard-working parents who no matter how intensely they struggled still weren't always able to pay the bills. Handwritten notes helped me get out of my small town and graduate from an Ivy League university when I really had no business being there. Handwritten notes brought me love and friendship beyond what I ever could have imagined for myself. And the philosophy of handwritten notes helped me run a successful business while being a full-time mom to three kids under three. And the best part about this was I went to bed each night happy and fulfilled knowing I lifted up other people above myself every single day.

I stand by it: handwritten notes filled my life with joy and abundance.

I know that through reading this book and putting its ideas in action, it can do the same for you.

(Signed, Carrie Pierce)

Chapter One

The Problem with Technology

When I was younger, my father and I drove through his-toric Pennsylvania, marveling at stone houses and old farms, a thowback to a time before cell phones, when folks went about their day unconcerned with social media or online extreme news of the day. There was something so soothing and comforting about those historic farms and homes. Their wide porches and grand shade trees were reminiscent of a simpler time when people would sit in rocking chairs lost in thought, wondering what their neighbors might be doing or simply watching the clouds float by while they shaped the meaning of their day. They could pray and ponder on loved ones and friends and maybe even write them a note or two before dinner, which they would eat at the table surrounded by their families, not a screen in sight.

This may sound idyllic and we all know our simple lives of the past weren't perfect and, in many respects, today's technological advancements have improved our lives in important and significant ways. I'll be the first to agree that technology has had an overall positive impact. All the same it's become quite obvious that technology has hijacked our focus. The rapid speed and artificiality of digital communication—especially on social media—has encouraged a mindset of self-focus and reactive anxious behaviors. Before phones and computers, we spent time reflecting. We took the time to muse not only about our own lives, but about friends and family. When was the last time you sat down with a cup of coffee and thought deeply about other people? Where did our built-in times for reflection go?

> There's beauty in thought. The act of sitting down to just sincerely appreciate another human being is a beautiful concept.

Nowadays, even when we have free time, we're distracted by tablets, phones, texts, emails, streaming, games, and on and on. In uncomfortable moments, in our "dead" space, we distract ourselves with clicks on our phones. Multi-tasking is chronic. Our waiting periods are now occupied with screens, not thought. While we're in the grocery line, sitting on the porch with our morning coffee, or waiting for dinner to come out of the oven, we are scrolling, filling our lives with distraction after distraction. We're hyper-focused on how we compare to others, judging ourselves based on social media posts, perpetuating our anxiety and an unhealthy "never-good-enough" mindset. When waiting for a friend at a restaurant we surf on our phones rather than think about the friend we're about to see. Can't sleep? We turn to our phones, anything rather than being alone with our thoughts. There's an over-reliance on online dating apps which cause people to rule in and rule out people on the basis of stats and not on the basis of any substantial human connection. And I would be the most hypocritical person in the world if I didn't admit to being guilty of much of what's described above. The momentum propelling us forward into digital numbness is almost unstoppable. According to a recent Nielsen report, American adults spend over eleven hours per day "listening to, watching, reading or generally interacting with media."[1] How do we even have time to grab a quick meal with those kinds of numbers? Of course, the answer is that usually, we don't even put our devices down while we eat.

We've lost sight of true human interaction, and the consequence is loneliness. A University of Pittsburgh study found a link between social media use and depression.[2] The study goes on to suggest the association is strong enough that clinicians could consider asking their patients with depression and anxiety about social media use. A separate study at the University of Arizona found that smartphone dependency led to increased loneliness.[3] Headlines like, "How tech and social media are making us feel lonelier than ever,"[4] are so common, that a search for "loneliness" and "technology" returns over forty-four million results.

....

1   Nielsen Website, "Time Flies: U.S. Adults Now Spend Nearly Half a Day Interacting with Media," July 31, 2018, https://www.nielsen.com/us/en/insights/article/2018/time-flies-us-adults-now-spend-nearly-half-a-day-interacting-with-media/.

2   Lin LY, Sidani JE, Shensa A, Radovic A, Miller E, Colditz JB, Hoffman BL, Giles LM, Primack BA. Association Between Social Media Use and Depression Among U.S. Young Adults. Depress Anxiety. 2016 Apr;33(4):323-31. doi: 10.1002/da.22466. Epub 2016 Jan 19. PMID: 26783723; PMCID: PMC4853817.

3   Alexis Blue, "New research suggests a person's reliance on his or her smartphone predicts greater loneliness and depressive symptoms, as opposed to the other way around," Sept. 30, 2019, https://news.arizona.edu/story/which-comes-first-smartphone-dependency-or-depression.

4   Leslie Katz, "How tech and social media are making us feel lonelier

The isolation of the COVID pandemic pushed us even further into our technological abyss and thus into solitude as face-to-face contact was replaced by virtual meetings, virtual classrooms, and FaceTime gatherings. According to one Gallup poll, before the pandemic just over 4% of American workers worked exclusively from home. During the pandemic, that figure rose to 43%. For white collar workers, the numbers were even starker, with 63% working from home.[5] I fear we've adapted a little too well, and the isolating, work-from-home trend could be permanent for many. Indeed, it's becoming clear that many of these people will never go back, as 76% of these workers say their employers will allow remote work to continue as the pandemic wanes. In other words, we have even more time to stare into our screens and less to interact with the outside world.

> While we can't ignore the benefits of working from home, we should also take the time to look back to identify and hold onto the old ways that still serve us well. The question becomes: How do we get our focus back to real life, to real people, to the place where real connections are made, and loneliness is thwarted?

than ever," June 18, 2020, https://www.cnet.com/culture/features/how-tech-and-social-media-are-making-us-feel-lonelier-than-ever/.

5 By Lydia Saad And Ben Wigert, Ph.D., "Remote Work Persisting and Trending Permanent," October 31, 2021, Gallup Website, https://news.gallup.com/poll/355907/remote-work-persisting-trending-permanent.aspx.

I'd personally love to spend hours on those porches my father and I passed on our drive back through history, not a phone in sight, waiting for the sound of Mom's dinner bell. But nostalgia, looking back alone, isn't really helpful. Nor is blindly jumping to the future. We need to be intentional about finding ways to weave the old fashioned with the new, to bring real human connection into our world as it is. How can we find a way in our modern world to forge those deep connections we've lost? To look back at what still works and benefits us?

We need to start with the small things.

I would posit that handwritten notes are one of those small things. And they have big impact.

The difference a note makes

> "I've learned that people will forget what you said, people will forget what you did, but people will never forget how you made them feel." —MAYA ANGELOU

One of the greatest things about simpler times was hand-written notes, and the good news is that not much has changed—a great handwritten note still occupies a special place in people's hearts. When you get one in the mail you ignore everything else that came in the mailbox that day and go directly to that note. You can almost hear the writer's voice as you read their hand-written word. Those letters are nourishing. They fill the heart and the soul with connection, and thus joy. If the note is written well enough, you'll be drawn to the sender in a way you'll remember for a long time to come.

But why is that? Why is a note in your own handwriting with your own well-thought-out words so intimate? How does it hit the emotions in a way a text never could? Partly, it happens because it's rare and more likely to become something people will remember for weeks to come—years to come if the note is carefully crafted. After all, when is the last time you've written or received a hand-written note? According to one study of over 2,000 people, one-third of them had not written anything by hand in the previous six months.[6]

But there's more to notes than scarcity. In fact, there's science.

Digital vs pen and paper

Multiple studies show that when we read on paper, as opposed to screen, our understanding and connection to the words increases.[7] Writing by hand is also more beneficial than typing as it leads to a deeper understanding of the subject we're writing about.[8] In addition, as Roland Jouvent, head of adult psychiatry at Pitié-Salpêtrière hospital in Paris explained to *The Guardian,* "Each person's hand is differ-

....

6   Anne Chemin, "Handwriting vs typing: is the pen still mightier than the keyboard?", December 16, 2014, theguardian.com/science/2014/dec/16/cognitive-benefits-handwriting-decline-typing.

7   Just one example of this phenomenon is this study: Pablo Delgado, Cristina Vargas, Rakefet Ackerman, Ladislao Salmerón,
Don't throw away your printed books: A meta-analysis on the effects of reading media on reading comprehension,
Educational Research Review, Volume 25, 2018, Pages 23-38.

8   Mueller PA, Oppenheimer DM. The Pen Is Mightier Than the Keyboard: Advantages of Longhand Over Laptop Note Taking. *Psychological Science.* 2014;25(6):1159-1168. doi:10.1177/0956797614524581

ent: the gesture is charged with emotion, lending it a special charm." In other words, "With handwriting, we come closer to the intimacy of the author."[9]

But there's more to handwritten notes than the physical act of putting pen to paper that makes them special.

> It's more than just the actual note, there's the act of thinking about other people. Note writing forces us to do this—to stop and think about what makes a person unique and special.

Taking the Time to Focus

The process of writing a note begins way before you actually write the note. It begins with turning off technology and sitting down to think about another person in a focused and thoughtful way. Clear your mind and focus only on them-- really see them and witness them. This is not necessarily an easy task. It can be *hard* to think of someone else, to think of something to write in a note. Recently one summer my mother helped a great deal with my three daughters and I decided write her a note to show my appreciation. I set my devices aside and sat with my pen and paper and made a list about what made her unique: her kindness, her generosity, her patience. Then, I thought of examples because it's important to be specific in letters. Once I conjured in my mind a few examples, I wrote the note, telling her how much I loved seeing her at her best as a grandma

---

9 Anne Chemin, *Guardian.*

and how I loved watching the joy on my girls' faces before they even walked in the door to her house just knowing what was about to come.

Writing that note forced me to connect with my mother in a way a quick heart-emoji text never could. By the time I was done writing, I was literally smiling. When she read the note, I knew she'd be smiling, too. She would cherish and look back at it over and over, and maybe even keep it forever. It would never disappear into an endless email in-box. It would never be just another text with the dozens of others she'd gotten that day.

Here's the best part: writing that note brought me joy, too. Thinking about her goodness and telling her why she matters made me feel better, the way focusing on the joyous side of life always does.

But don't just take my word for it. In the next chapter, we'll look at examples from history and from modern day life that show how just the act of putting down our technology, thinking of others, and then telling them what we've thought with a hand-written note really can lead us from loneliness to connection.

Chapter Two

Why Old-Fashioned Notes Aren't So Old Fashioned

My personal attachment to hand-written notes came as a result of experiencing their power throughout my life. Growing up with blue collar parents is an education in itself. Dad worked in a warehouse—the Allen Envelope Company warehouse. Mom was a waitress. The philosophy that you put your head down, do your best, be humble, and try to be a good citizen was ingrained in me from a very young age.

One thing I noticed growing up was that everybody seemed to love my dad. He was just that kind of guy with a million friends. On any given Sunday, you might find him helping a neighbor cut down trees, helping a friend paint their house or coaching football for the local Pop Warner team. Whatever he was doing, he would notice things about people that made them special and great—the kind of things other people would overlook. And he would make a special point to mention it to that person. He was naturally curious in others and made sure to tell them of their good traits. By watching him, I got into the habit of doing the same.

Mom and Dad both had a way of seeing the positive in situations. In my Grandmother's final years, she started to lose her filter the way old people sometimes do. At times it was comical but other times inappropriate comments carried the potential of hurting others. And because of this my dad was one of the few people willing to take her out for lunch and to get her hair and nails done. He knew what he was in for with her brutal comments to strangers, but he also knew it made her feel special—my dad's highest goal.

When Dad took her out to eat, she would complain about, well pretty much everything—the temperature of the food, not enough salt, no ketchup on the table, and on and on. Did my father complain about any of this? No. He looked at the positive: how great the salad was that day, how nice it was to be together, how good a cook she is and the food she used to make for him. At some point during the meal, my dad would sneak off to the back of the restaurant to give the waitress an extra-large tip and to apologize. He'd say, "I'm sorry. You don't deserve to be treated that way. You have been handling her really great, by the way." By the time they left the restaurant, my father had made his impact. What could have been a horrible day for the waitress ended on a good note because my father had acknowledged her and thought through what the experience was like for her. My grandmother felt great because she'd been treated with kindness. But here is where I want you to pay attention: my dad felt great too, maybe the best, because sincerely thinking of others gives you an internal lift like no other feeling. His heart was a little fuller than before and he succeeded in turning a difficult situation into a positive experience.

Call it charisma or call it what you want, my Dad just had that way about him that made him and everyone around him happy. People were drawn to him like bees to honey because he made everybody feel like they mattered.

It was just who he was. He was constantly looking at what the world was like from other people's perspectives. I started to notice other people around me like my dad who had the same energy. I watched how they were in the world, and realized I wanted to also have that positive energy. Somewhere along the road, through seeing my dad and others who acted as he did, I picked up on the power of that philosophy and put it into practice in my daily life. For me, this attitude translated into my practice of writing handwritten notes.

The Science Behind Kindness

There is a lot of scientific research to explain why this way of being in the world makes everyone around you, including yourself, happier. In his book, *Altruism: The Power of Compassion to Change Yourself and the World,* researcher Ricard Matthieu explains, "actively focusing on caring mindfulness and compassion can physically alter the structure of our brains." His research shows that "caring mindfulness meditation" increases the volume of grey matter in our brains. It makes the hippocampus—the region of the brain associated with positive emotion, long term memory, and the autonomic nervous system—more active. It also reduces the activity and size of the amygdala, the area of the brain associated with stress, anxiety, and depression.

Matthieu was a French researcher with a PhD in molecular biology who was so affected by his research, he became a Buddhist monk and later the French interpreter for the Dalai Lama. But you don't have to become a Buddhist monk or even a person who meditates to experience the benefits of altruism. Matthieu showed that while it's true that experts can achieve greater structural changes in the brain, while novices showed far less, people don't need to be lifetime practitioners of intense meditation to feel the positive effects of altruism. "Even meditating on caring mindfulness for twenty minutes a day can produce great benefits," he says. "Even ten seconds of wishing another person well works." The goal is to spend as much time as you can focusing on good thoughts about others. The more time you spend "focused on altruistic thoughts," the more your brain will structurally change.[10] Matthieu shows that simply wishing people well can create individual and societal benefits. He calls this "the banality of goodness":

> It's what we do every day, giving someone a smile, helping an elderly person, taking underprivileged kids on an afternoon holiday. It's not so difficult. There are so many unsung heroes of altruism, people who do 'ordinary goodness' and we don't pay enough attention to that. It's not in the news, but there is always good woven into the fabric of our lives, and we must pay more attention to that and also be part of it.

The key point to remember about altruism according to Matthieu is that you have to mean it. To just wish someone well in order to make your own brain better doesn't work. "You have to actually feel the warm-heartedness," he says. "You need caring mindfulness, you can't just be mindful— after all, you can be a mindful sniper. You must imbue mindfulness with a sense of benevolence and care."

....
10 Matthieu Ricard speaks at TED Global 2014, South, Session 12 – Might Spaces, October 5-10, 2014, Rio de Janeiro, Brazil. Photo: James Duncan Davidson/TED

Weaving altruism into our lives

"Altruism is innate, but its not instinctual. Everybody's wired for it, but a switch has to be flipped."
—WRITER AND POET DAVID ROKOFF

Finding everyday ways to build altruism in your life is a powerful habit. How do we incorporate this in a world of technological and physical disconnect? It's all very well and good for me to say, "Be altruistic" or "do ordinary goodness." But how exactly do you drive home that habit so that it becomes a part of your life—and thus part of your brain? Researchers on habit formation have done a great deal of research to answer that question.

Creating habits is not complicated, but it does take planning. The first step of forming a habit is always to set a specific goal. "Doing ordinary goodness" is not specific enough.

Once you've set your specific goal, the second step to forming a habit is to create a specific plan. "Thinking about others in a positive way" isn't a specific plan. However, "sitting down to think about one person every Friday for twenty minutes in order to write one meaningful note to them," is an excellent way to manifest the habit of altruism and thinking good thoughts about others in your life.

The third step to habit-forming is to make it enjoyable. Writing and sending notes can be a beautiful experience if you invest in beautiful paper, pens, envelopes, and stamps. Sending the note can feel energizing. And getting excited feedback from the people who get your notes is the best part of all.

In 1928 psychologist William Moulton Marston created the theory behind DiSC, later adapted by Walter Clarke into the Activity Vector Analysis. It was a way to assess what drives a person's personality. "D" is dominance and drive.. "I" is influence and social acceptance. "S" is support and steadiness. And "C" is cautious and careful. When I took the DiSC test, I was 100% "D." The man who administered the test flipped out because he had never seen 100% D in anyone and had never seen a score even close to that in a female. I tell this story because the assessment wasn't inaccurate. Being a driver personality, I tend to get hyper focused on activities that give me the best overall return on my life and career goals in relation to time spent. And I found that the ritual of note writing provided me the best return. This philosophy tripled my income and won me business awards. More importantly, I went to bed each night with a full heart and a feeling of humility and integrity. A lot of people think that altruism and note writing is fufu and silly. It isn't. The process of writing notes is one of the key things that you can do to fundamentally manifest connection, joy, and happiness in your life.

The difference between ritual, routine, and habit

Note writing can be a habit, just like brushing your teeth or putting on your seatbelt. Think of it as a muscle you work out, develop and that becomes stronger over time. This is something you do regularly, but takes more effort when you're first getting started. Only by setting up a routine can you begin to alter the way you operate in the world. Rituals are routines endowed with a specific attitude. As you'll see in future chapters and as Matthieu teaches, that specific attitude has to be altruistic, thinking of everyone else and never of yourself. When you mix habit and ritual, you have truly created a way of being in a world that can bring connection and happiness without thought. Note writing can be the first step to lead you to ritual.

Note writing in my life:
connection, joy, and abundance.

My life has been a prime example of Matthieu's philosophy in action as manifested in the practice of writing notes. There are many examples you'll see throughout this book, but here, I'll tell you just one story about my acceptance into college at the University of Pennsylvania. My parents told me there was no way they could pay for it. They were already stretched thin and stressed about money, and I had a basketball scholarship at another school. But I had set my sights on the Ivy League, I wasn't sure I could get in with just a 990 on my SATS competing against so many other high achievers. And in truth, I probably shouldn't have gotten in based on my grades and my scores. But I decided that if I got in, I'd figure out how to pay for it myself, so I applied.

After I applied, I'd call the admissions office every day, just to check if any decisions had been made. I felt so bad for the woman who had to answer the phone. I would apologize when I called, but I knew I couldn't express my gratitude fully over the phone while she was busy and distracted with a million other calls, while I was full of anxiety over my own situation. So after I got off the phone, I wrote her a note telling her how much I appreciated her and appreciated how hard her job must be with people like me calling all the time. I wrote that I was sorry to trouble her so much, that I understood she must be sick of me. I was very focused on honoring her time and being respectful of her patience.

She wasn't the person who decided who got in and who didn't. I wasn't trying to influence her. I didn't want anything from my notes. I just wanted to say thank you properly, with real intention. I was raised to say thank you and be grateful. I hoped that she got a little joy out of my note, and that she forgave me for all my calls.

One day, she called me back. In an almost conspiring, secretive voice she said to me, "I've got news. I'm not supposed to tell you this, but you're in." To this day I'll never know if she impacted the acceptance decision, but I do know she was rooting for me and genuinely happy for me. I think I had to have been the only one to get a secret phone call ahead of time from the lady in the admissions office. We celebrated together over the phone. And as most people know, having someone to celebrate with is almost as important as the achievement itself.

This isn't a story about how to get into an Ivy League college. If you think it is, then you're missing the point of the story, of this chapter, and of the book. This is a story about how two strangers, alone in their own worlds, created a connection through a deeper regard for one another through note writing that brought joy. It was a beautiful moment in both our days. I had given her a feeling of importance that she probably didn't receive on a regular basis. It set me apart from the applicant masses. It probably made her look at her job a little differently, as someone who genuinely helped another person through an anxious time and was sincerely thanked for it.

> Living in this world can be fulfilling, one where we're all connected, where joy is abundant. But we are 100% responsible for creating it. Note writing is a small way to do just that.

Some might perceive note writing as scary. And certainly, it can be. What if you're not the kind of person who naturally reaches out to make those sorts of personal connections? Note writing for many people can sound as foreign as becoming a Buddhist monk. I get that. And that's why the next chapter introduces one of my heroes. A man of everyday advice that is meant for the "common man," for that person who isn't naturally talented at reaching out and spreading joy. His name is Dale Carnegie, his book is *How to Win Friends and Influence People,* and with his principles in mind, I am sure you will be able to act on altruism, no matter where you fall on the DiSC personality metric or how likely you are to pick up a phone or a pen and express true gratitude to another person.

Chapter Three

The Art of Personal Interaction

Dale Carnegie's *How to Win Friends and Influence People* sits on my desk with the spine both glued and taped together because it's been read so many times. I read it once a year at minimum. Not only is Carnegie's advice timeless but it also applies to multiple aspects of life. If I'm stuck on a problem, I read a few chapters to gain clarity on how to address it. And when I'm in a bad mood, the book offers perspective and meaning at a time when the big picture isn't so clear.

I'm not the only one who loves this book. Since Carnegie wrote it in 1936, it has sold over thirty million copies, making it one of the bestselling books of all time. Note that it's not one of the bestselling self-help books of all time, but *one of the overall best-selling books of all time.*

What do Dale Carnegie and his book have to do with writing notes? After all, Carnegie didn't have the issue of technology impeding people's authentic connections. Back in 1936, handwritten notes were much more common, as was personal interaction. Now, when we think about connecting with one another our interactions have been reduced to inauthentic on-line interactions and disruptive, reactive text messaging. The importance of recognizing the added dangers of screens, texting, and coldness is when we think about connecting with one another cannot be overstated.

Dale Carnegie's philosophy is not just for the olden days, it is a timeless and effective approach on interacting with people face to face.

Carnegie had two specific goals in mind: sincerely making others feel like they matter and influencing people. To truly understand the philosophy of note writing, you must lead with the other person's good traits at the forefront. You can't aim to manipulate or self-serve if you're going to experience true joy and connection. As a bonus, success and winning just so happen to go hand in hand with the philosophy of leading with sincere and altruistic thinking.

If you read Carnegie closely enough, you'll see that he was after exactly what I'm after when I write handwritten notes—true, human connection—but that in 1936, they didn't have the language or culture for expressing *abundance, intention,* and *connection* the way we do now. So, while Carnegie's title focused his readers on the results of the process, his methods are the same as mine and **so is the final goal of authentic connection.** Another way to think of it is that the note writing philosophy puts the emphasis on *friends* and *people* instead of on *win* and *influence,* but it's all there in the title and always has been.

> **By following Carnegie's principles, you are fundamentally changing the way you are in the world, and this changes your results, even if that's not the goal.**

This may be confusing, so let's dive into Carnegie's big ideas one-by-one and adapt them to the small act of writing handwritten notes. By the end of this chapter, you'll see how following Carnegie's ideas and shifting the nuances of intention will give you an impactful, *modern* way to act on Carnegie's big ideas.

Let's look at the six steps of Dale Carnegie's *How to Win Friends and Influence People* and apply his methods to train yourself how to write a powerful and engaging note.

In the end you could find yourself with more "wins" and more influence. But remember that's not the point nor the goal of the note writing ritual. The goal is to deepen your relationships, lift others up and get back to what authentic relationships are foundationally built on.

Six Steps to Connection

An adaptation of this applied to note writing could be what Carnegie calls, "Six Ways to Make People Like You." I call it, "Six Ways to Connect on a Deep and Meaningful Level." They're very simple but not necessarily easy.

1. Become genuinely interested in other people.
2. Smile.
3. Remember that a person's name is to that person the sweetest and most important sound in any language.
4. Be a good listener. Encourage others to talk about themselves.
5. Talk in terms of the other person's interests.
6. Make the other person feel important—and do it sincerely.

Carnegie's points are straightforward and powerful, but they're also broad, and perhaps hard to act on. How exactly do you go out in the world and make someone feel important? How exactly can you be a good listener? Carnegie offers us some wise & insightful tips. Let's go through them one by one.

ONE: "Become genuinely interested in other people."

You must show sincere interest in other people if you know you're going to write them a note with impact or else your note will get tossed aside as "oh that was nice." What we are after is the lingering thoughts that capture the other person's attention so deeply and significantly that they think about it for weeks. They show it to friends, they talk about it and proudly display it. For a lot of people, this concept is very difficult because most people spend much of their time thinking of themselves or distracting themselves from real thought without even realizing it. This isn't a criticism. I'll be the first to admit I'm guilty of overindulging in distractions. It's simply human nature. Most of us worry to no end about what others think of us. And most of us are starving for a genuine sense of appreciation.

I remember taking a client and her friend out to see homes and one of the things she really wanted was a bathtub. The friend then responded with, "I hate bathtubs, ugh sitting there alone with my thoughts, thinking about all the ways I've messed up seems awful." Her comment was noteworthy because most people are afraid to be alone with their thoughts, they're thoughts are too often spent second guessing themselves and worrying about what other people think. *How does everybody see me? What do they think of me?*

That's when they grab their phone and start playing games, watching videos, clicking through the internet or reassuring themselves and the world that they're life is great by posting social media pictures and posts.

The best way to get out of this lonely cycle of self-doubt is to spend time, and I mean a LOT of time, thinking of others. Preparing to write notes creates an almost ritualistic, concrete process to do this. It gives you a more productive space to be with your thoughts. When you plan to write that note you should turn off your devices, take a seat and think about what makes another person great. You might drift off into thinking about what's lousy about them too, but train yourself to cast negative thoughts away, substituting with positive appreciative thoughts. The mind is like a muscle and if you train it enough you'll get stronger and better at this skill. Reflect on what makes another human being important, think about what you genuinely appreciate about them.

Keeping yourself mindful of others and where they might get their feeling of importance is what high-impact note writing is all about.

TWO: "Smile"

Carnegie points out that, "a smile says, 'I like you. You make me happy. I am glad to see you.'" (HWFIP, 69) But what do you do when you can't be there in person to say all that with your smile?

I bet you know the answer already: send a note.

> A handwritten note is a smile at another
> person when you can't be there.

I keep a box filled with notes that other people have written to me. When I need a pick-me-up or even when I have a spare minute, I'll pull them out and take a peek. They make me smile just the way I smile back at a person who smiles at me. Studies show that all this smiling actually makes you happier because it increases levels of the hormones dopamine and serotonin.

By sending your notes out into the world, you're actually sending your smiles out in the world.

For many people who are shy, it's a way to smile from afar. For people who had missed the opportunity to smile in person because they were preoccupied with whatever it was they were doing, it's a way to make that right. And for everyone, a note is a way to preserve the effect of smiling beyond the moment.

THREE: "Remember that a person's name is to that person the sweetest and most important sound in any language."

My twin daughters take music lessons from a man married to a woman from Japan who didn't speak much English. At Christmas, we gave them a small gift to thank them for all the kindness they showed my daughters. Naturally, I wrote a note to go along with it, and when I wrote her name, I used Japanese characters. Google translator assisted here and I did the best I could, although I imagine that it probably looked like something a child had written. Still, this was a case of how modern technology isn't all bad. It still can assist us with the old-fashioned process of connection, but only if we use it in the service of greater human connection.

Did she care that maybe my note wasn't perfect? No, not at all. In fact, I got a heartfelt thank you from the family, their thank you for my thank you note stressed how much it meant to his wife that I wrote her name in Japanese. And his wife commented we might be the "the perfect family." Amazing because she hadn't known much about our family, yet this is the high regard she had for us after writing a thoughtful note that stepped into her world and made her feel like her uniqueness was a big deal. Now, I guarantee you, there is nothing even close to perfect about my family or my Japanese writing. But that didn't matter because she was touched that I tried. I honored her by taking the time to write her name in terms that were meaningful to her.

Another great thing about writing handwritten notes is they always include people's names—once on the envelope, again on the note itself. People love the sound and the sight of their names, especially when it's written in someone's personalized handwriting.

Many people have trouble remembering names. Carnegie explains, "Most people don't remember names for the simple reason that they don't take the time and energy necessary to concentrate and repeat and fix names indelibly in their minds." (HWFIP, P 84) When you know that you're going to write a note later, it forces you to take the time to find out people's names and commit them to memory. I write them down, either on my phone or on a scrap of paper to put into my phone later. I also ask how to spell their names if I don't already know—there's nothing wrong with asking. In fact, asking shows people that you're interested in them. It shows you're paying attention and thinking a little deeper about them. Especially with a foreign name, pause and ask, "How do you spell that?" You'll find that people like to tell you. You've shown that you care.

FOUR: "Be a good listener. Encourage others to talk about themselves."

When you know you're going to write a person a note later, you alter the dynamic of the interaction. You sharpen your focus on the other person. It awakens your curiosity in them. Did they wake up having to take care of sick parents or sick kids? How is their spouse doing? How is their career going? What was their career anyway? If we listen to others a little more, not only can we write a more impactful note, but we develop more patience and a desire to connect with someone not because we want something from them, but because we want to offer them the incredible feeling of being witnessed in one of their best lights. They really do matter in this world.

This is powerful stuff. Cultivating this strong of a connection and spiritual elevation means sincerely listening to others. Give them the stage and don't trump it. Avoid the self-relating trap whereby you bring the conversation back to yourself justifying that you're relating to the other person, when in actuality you've stolen their stage. A few years ago, I took on a role as an Executive Leadership Coach and I found that even with top level executives this is often the hardest point to digest. The focus must rest entirely in their world and in their space. Self-relating might seem like you're in their world but that's just it, you're "in" their world thinking you're boosting the conversation when really, you're weakening their status. Rather than chiming in about yourself, let the conversation hover completely on them.

Often, when we're face-to-face, we're too rushed to have that real conversation. Taking the time to think about another person, even when they're not there, is another way to "listen." You're going back over everything you noticed about them: did their hair look especially great today? What was that they said about their mom? Or their garden? You'll be surprised that when you see the person next, you'll have questions at the ready because you've been thinking about them. In this way, writing notes goes beyond the note itself to improve your real-time interactions, your way of being in the world.

FIVE: "Talk in terms of the other person's interests."

Carnegie writes that "dealing with people is probably the biggest problem you'll face, especially if you're in business." I agree, and not just in business, but in life, too. The reason it's a problem, though, isn't other people. It's you. Most people approach life hyper focused on what they want from others. Through writing notes, you're breaking down that framework of *me against them*. Now, it's *me with you*, it's *me wanting to know more about you*.

Giving the other person the stage, talking in terms of what they like and leaving the conversation completely on them will make the other person feel important. But only if you do it sincerely. If you really aren't into orchestras then don't mention how much you admire they're being in one. It is disingenuous and will fall flat. But perhaps you admire the work ethic they put into it. Perhaps, you admire their passion when speaking about it. Or maybe when they were talking to you, you noticed how intelligently the person spoke about the subject. When you plan on writing a note to someone with the sole intention of making them feel appreciated, you need to be sincere, and this requires an extra level of focus.

If you show up with your own needs and your own ego at the forefront, other people's feelings of importance are diminished. If your goal is to exert your own importance, then this book isn't for you. If you show up touting how much you already know about the subject and figure you'll maybe tell them a thing or two about it, you'll diminish the other person and build a wall of isolation between you both rather than cultivating the deeper connection. The nice thing about sitting down and writing notes is that you put aside your own needs and enlarge your world by figuring out how to deeply connect with another person. Sitting down and writing a letter means giving yourself time and space to be curious about another person and give them the proper amount of respect and observance that they deserve. It's like going back to the rocking chair with your coffee on the front porch and just thinking.

Then, when the thinking is done, you can act by writing the perfect note that focuses on them.

SIX: "Make the other person feel important—and do it sincerely."

I've operated my real estate business a little different than most realtors. I operated on the premise that I do not talk about myself. I've always tried to focus conversation on my clients with the intent to make my clients feel important. They're doing important things. They're leading exceptional lives. They each have their own success stories. They're lives matter and in their eyes their lives matter 100x more than my own. You don't make people feel important by droning on about yourself. Let's face it, people may ask about your kids out of politeness but they're not looking for a 10-minute answer. This part of the book is difficult to write because I do not like to brag, boast, or talk about myself. In fact, I wrote and erased this portion of the book multiple times. At the same time, just this once I'm going to share because it's important to illustrate how impactful this concept can really be. While I operated my business on the premise of focusing on other people, I managed to become the number one salesperson in the state at Coldwell Banker the same year I had 3 kids under 3 years old, put my husband at the time through full time business school and owned and managed 6 rental properties. I did virtually no marketing for my business and still pulled off almost $45 million in sales while turning multiple clients away. I rarely went on a client interview because I had more referrals than I could handle.

But the thing I'm most proud of is that my success never involved boasting or talking about myself to others. That would have gone against every grain of my being. I was raised to be humble. I must illustrate these successes in order to show you how well this philosophy works but mind you I've made nobody feel bigger by sharing it and other than making a point in this book I never share these details with anyone. The point of the story is to illustrate how making other people feel special and important will work wonders in both the business world and in your personal life.

Here's an example of how this played out: One time a couple's parents were coming to check out a house. They asked me about my background, how long I'd been in the business and if I owned any real estate myself. They were helping their son out with the down payment and naturally wanted to stay involved. Here's what I did. Instead of talking about myself, I took special note of what I appreciated about the buyers and the parents, and later, I sent a note to the parents. I don't recall exactly what verbiage I used but it went something like this: *Mr. and Mrs. Smith, you should be proud. Your son has more discipline at 27 than most of my other clients have at 50. He's gone about the process, asking incredibly intelligent questions and making smart, well-informed decisions along the way. And he handles stress like a pro. Good job, mom and dad.*

These parents, who only met me one time, turned out to be a big source of referrals even though they never directly worked with me. They might not have any idea personally how I operate as a realtor but having impacted them with the handwritten note, they felt seen and appreciated. And they perceived me to be a smarter realtor because of it.

Was I expecting anything in return from them? I hope you know the answer to that by now: absolutely not. I wrote the note because I like to make people feel special. As a nice side bonus, it brought me business. Never write a note while thinking, *I want to make money.* Instead think, *I love the feeling of making other people feel good and lifting them up by focusing on what is important to them.* You might be surprised by the results.

Next Steps: Making It Real

The last three chapters laid out the background thinking about why the philosophy of handwritten notes works and why it matters. They discussed the problems of technology and how they can hold us back from true connection to bring us only loneliness. They analyzed the science behind handwriting vs. typing, and notes vs. email and other digital forms of connection. They introduced some important thinkers, including Ricard Matthieu, Dale Carnegie, and my parents, who showed me how to carry myself in the world and why. But now, it's time to actually get started. Let's write some notes. The next chapter will make the case that by following four simple steps, you'll be a champion note writer in no time. I'm excited for you to get started—and then to see the results of powerful connections, abundance, and joy.

Chapter Four

The Ritual of Writing the
(Not So) Perfect Note

In my days of being a realtor, there were often situations where multiple offers were made on a home. At the market peak, sellers' agents might be looking at twenty or more offers. My buyers' offers needed to stand out against the rest. I'd been on the other side of the transaction enough times to know the strategies other realtors would employ to "win" the multiple offer situation. Offer price and terms were of course factors but mostly it involved bragging about how great their buyer clients were and boasting about how great they were as agents.

Bragging and boasting weren't my thing, so I adopted a different approach. Operating on the philosophy from this book, I spent a lot of time thinking in terms of the world of the seller's agent and the sellers. Generally speaking, luxury market realtors and sellers tend to value their time, poise, and reputation more than most other things. So, my conversations and message to the seller's agent would focus on how hard I knew they'd been working and how I understood that dealing with multiple offers was stressful. Picking the right offer out of 20+ offers as a seller's agent was no easy task. If I knew the agent personally, I would add something to my sentiments about what I specifically appreciated about that particular agent and how the opportunity to do a transaction with someone of their caliber would be an honor. And that they deserved to choose a buyer who would maintain their high caliber way of operating. I would end the letter by saying that if they picked my client's offer, we were going to ensure their reputation, a low stress transaction, and we'd fix any potential obstacles with minimal to no time/effort on their part wherever possible. We were going to ensure that they and their seller wouldn't have one thing to worry about because we understood how much they're having to deal with and we would not put anything further on their plate than what was absolutely necessary to close the transaction. More often than not, we would win the house.

Often times we weren't the best bid but won anyway, seller agents would say, "Carrie, your clients didn't put in the best offer, but we really wanted to work with you, so you got it." Other times when the terms were close, agents would call and tell me what we would need to do to win the offer. For example, one client bid on a $1.2 million house on the south side of Seattle in a highly desirable area. The seller's agent called me and said that my clients would have to go to $1.3 if they wanted the house. They said, "We don't want to work with these other agents. We want to work with you." So I went back to my clients, and I said, "This is your opportunity if you want this house." My clients didn't come up to 1.3M but they came close and we won anyway.

You might be thinking how hypocritical it is to tell you about this when I've said I don't like to boast. Admittedly, I spent hours second guessing the inclusion of these passages in the book. In the end, I felt the need to illustrate how humility and thinking of others is very powerful beyond the endorphins and filling of the soul. The stories are testaments to that power. This approach can be a tremendous business asset. At risk of being repetitive, it can't be stressed enough: if you're doing the ritual to receive something in return, then you aren't getting the point of this book. Whether you win business or not, you've made another human feel good. Even if I didn't win an offer, I felt good knowing I made another hard-working agent feel as if they sincerely mattered.

Whether in real estate or in another type of business, too often people think success requires substantial self-promotion. They market themselves having no idea that it lands tiresome to others. This was never my style, I focused and diverted back focus on the person I was dealing with. When clients asked about me or my successes, I would give a quick, humble answer and immediately turn back the conversation to them. The mortgage representative I worked with would say, "Carrie, every time clients work with you, you get them a house so quickly while everybody else is spinning their wheels. I don't know how you do it." I'll bet most people wouldn't think humility and "other focused" thinking would have such an impact. How do you explain this to someone who wants to know your secret sauce? If I answered, *"It takes humility and spending a ton of time thinking of others,"* they probably wouldn't understand.

That being said, I knew how I did it. It was the philosophy I'd internalized by writing handwritten notes. I wasn't focusing on the other agent because I wanted to win. I wasn't doing it to be successful. I was doing it to focus honestly and sincerely on them as people so that I could build relationships and bring more joy and abundance into their lives. I focused on expressing one thought: *Here's what I know about you that makes you great.* I did it so that I could be a better person in the world by making the world better for others. Winning bidding wars and real estate success was a great fringe benefit, but it was beside the point. The primary goal was to make a deep, positive impact on others.

> **Note writing is a way of life whereby you're training yourself to think about the other person.**

When you understand how deep you have to go to write a successful note—one that lifts another person up—you understand that getting into the correct mindset doesn't start when you pick up a pen and paper, and it doesn't end when you sign your name and send it out into the world. It starts with sincerity and wholehearted thinking about the other person and ends with making them feel valuable. The first time you set out to do this, it may take a long time and it may be difficult. In fact, if it's not difficult then you're probably not doing it right. Don't phone it in, you must fully take the leap into another person's world and think of what you appreciate about them. So be prepared that the first few times may be a struggle. But like anything, the more you practice doing it the right way, the better you get. You'll even start to enjoy it so much that after a while, you won't need to schedule it into your day or into your business plan. You'll do it naturally and it will become a habit. But like all habits, it takes intentional training. Don't get discouraged if it takes you a while in the beginning. It's probably a good indication that you're doing it right.

STEP 1: Set aside the time and the space

Mark Twain once said, "I didn't have time to write you a short letter, so I wrote you a long one." What he meant was that if you're not spending the time to really think about what you want to say, you're just going to drone on and on, and the result will be lackluster. Instead of spouting off with long-winded superlatives, set aside dedicated time to really think about why the other person matters so that you can accurately get to the point.

Time and intentionality are key. Slow down your world and allow yourself space to process what makes the other person great. In this way, sitting down to write a note is a good processing ritual. If you want to feel deeper connections, less alone, and you want to fill your soul with goodness, you need to force everything else out. This requires time and intention. Turn your phone and laptop off. Find a quiet, distraction-free space to sit with your thoughts.

As a working mother of three, I know how impossible this sounds. I'm not kidding when I say this is one of the hardest parts of writing notes. Setting aside time and space for anything is hard. But you must be committed and intentional. Add it to your business plan. Add it to your to-do list. Book it into your calendar in advance so nothing else gets in the way. It was in my business plan to write five notes a week. But what's important to note is that my five business notes weren't necessarily to a database or to five potential clients. That would be missing the point. They were any five people. If I couldn't come up with five people to write notes to one week, I doubled down and challenged myself—*I had to find five people.* Maybe, I'd write a note to my kids' teachers, to family, to nurses, or to neighbors. Maybe it was the music teacher for putting on a great performance at the concert. Or the mechanic who fixed my car. Or the woman who cut my hair. Sometimes it got really ridiculous—and fun. Maybe I'll write a note to my best friend from her cat, maybe I'll write a note to my daughter from the pretend monster in her closet. It was anyone I could think of, and it forced my creativity. It forced me out of my own head, to think of the lives of others and how I could make a positive and lasting impact.

STEP 2: Turn off your technology

I mentioned above and its worthy of emphasizing again: turn off your technology. Once I had chosen a person to write to and found the place and time, step two was leaving the digital world behind. The first place many people go when things are hard is clicking through the internet. Don't tempt yourself. Turn it off. There are circumstances where Facebook or Instagram may be appropriate. If I had forgotten a child's or pet's name I may go on social media. But unless absolutely necessary, turning social media off is part of this ritual.

One temptation is to visit someone's Facebook or social media page to catch up on their life, and then write a handwritten note about what you saw. I would argue against doing this. Here's why: chances are what you see about another person on social media is driven by insecurities. It may not represent reality to that person. It may even be associated with loneliness and depression by that person. If the goal is authentic connections, its best not to dignify a social media post that may be a false representation or portrayal of someone's persona, instead try and use your more direct dealings with the person to come up with something to write.

> **Stay away from technology and social media if possible. Remember, we're looking for deep connections here. These will never come from anything learned on social media.**

Turn off your TV, your phone, and your technology. Leave yourself with a blank canvas to paint a portrait of the other person the way you see them in the real world.

STEP 3: Ask yourself, *What makes this person great? Be specific.*

Now that you've made time and space to think without technology, it's time to really think and get specific about why the other person matters in this world. It can be helpful to create a list of all the things you love and appreciate about somebody. Here's a list that I just wrote this morning with my coffee while thinking about an old friend: *intuitive, quick to pick up on key details that really matter, unique ability to be "crazy fun" but also hold tight to her morals, patient.*

After I jot down a list, I take some time to look over and ask myself more questions. Where have I seen this person at their best? Which of these traits are most meaningful to the person? Which aren't really true and I'm reaching?

Where do I need to be more specific? The category *kindness* can encompass so much. How and when is she kind? Which category feels most true to the person? Maybe, one thing will just jump out at me as so true to the person, I can throw the rest away.

Once I find the traits I want to write about, I think: *well, how does that show up as great in their life?* Think of examples of specific things they've done that made you come up with the trait in the first place. It's hard because you have to be very precise and concrete. I want to write sentences that express, *here's when I've seen you be a pillar to those around you, and I was really impressed.* For example, in chapter one, I described writing a letter to my mother. This was the process behind that letter:

1. Make a list of attributes.
2. Think them through more by asking questions. I thought, *well, what did she do exactly that was so loving?* The letter I eventually wrote read: "... *I've seen you at your best as a grandma when I go to your house, and the kids immediately experience joy before they're even walking in the door, just knowing what's about to come, because they know that you're going to be so happy to see them ...* "

STEP 4: Uniqueness is key—and it goes both ways.

Before you start writing, remember that the reason you're writing is to make someone feel better about themselves. One of the best ways to do this is to focus on what makes them unique. For instance, I have a friend with cancer. She didn't deserve to be lumped together with everyone else who has cancer nor was a generic sentiment found on the internet appropriate for someone with as much spunk and fight in her like my friend. I thought about what makes her unique: *what makes her uniquely equipped to fight cancer?* How does she crave to be seen through this experience? *What will make her feel appreciated for who she is, not just as a person with cancer but as herself?*

The word I kept coming up with to describe her was *fearless*. But even fearless can be a generic sounding term. I didn't want her lumped together with other fearless people going through cancer. I wanted her to know she was unique and special in her own way different from everyone else. What exactly about her showed her fearlessness in a unique way? Well, for one, she refused to call herself a patient. She also refused to let her diagnosis get her down or get in her way of everyday life. She was fighting, but she was still the same kick-ass, funny person she had always been. And she went out of her way to help other people even more than she wanted help for herself. This felt very specific to her, so I wrote: *You, Liz Larsen, are fighting cancer more fiercely than anyone else I know. And you're setting this inspiring example for your kids while they're watching how you tackle cancer will your unstoppable mindset. In fact, I kind of feel bad for the cancer.*

Joking about cancer might not seem "proper," but in this case, it was exactly right because I had thought specifically about her and who she uniquely was: a fun, kick-butt person who just happened to have cancer. I couldn't have written that final line to just anyone. It took the letter from general to specific. I hope I made her feel that if anyone could beat cancer on this earth, it would be her.

This is an important example of how your notes should not just be unique to the other person, but unique to yourself, too. Your notes can be fun if you're fun. Or sweet if you're sweet. The key is that they shouldn't sound as if just anyone else could have written them. Use your personality to lift the other person up, to give them a little of your energy, and to pile on your support in your own way. People are craving real connections in this world. To not feel alone, they must know that they are real and seen, and that you are a real and present witness to their life.

STEP 5: Stop worrying about grammar, handwriting, or the perfect paper.

....

I often joke that my "dumbness" is one of my best qualities. Joking aside, it's true. In addition to dumbing down to stay curious about people and leaving the stage open for them, in my notes, you'll find a ton of grammar mistakes. My writing style isn't fluid or perfect, but I don't let it stop me from sending the note. English teachers aside, if you think a person is going to be more concerned with grammar, than telling them how uniquely great they are, then you're shorting yourself of a more enjoyable way of being in the world, and so are they.

Do not focus on note perfection to the point of never sending the note.

Remember, you're thinking about the other person, not yourself and your flaws and limitations. You're thinking about how they're experiencing your note on the receiving end. You're only concerned with: *have I given this person the proper amount of thought?* If you really sat down and considered that person and what makes them extra special, all that will come through in your card, no matter how shoddy your sentence structure or how cheesy you think it sounds. I promise you, they won't notice, and if they do, they won't care. In fact, you may have even drawn them closer to you by showing your own vulnerability.

That's not to say that you want the note to look a mess. If I look back at what I've written, and it has so many cross-outs that it looks like I didn't care when writing it, I'll write it again. Because I'm a terrible writer, I often end up with rough drafts. The point I'm making here is that at some point you may have to say to yourself, *this is good enough. I got my point across.* When writing a note for business, you might be more careful with handwriting, grammar, and spelling mistakes. My point is, don't worry so much about your own flaws that you fail to send out good vibes to the recipient. Perfection isn't necessary.

STEP 6: Reviewing what you wrote— the 80%-20% rule

Congratulations! Your note is done. But you still have a few more quick steps before you send it off. First, make sure you followed the 80%-20% rule: is the note 80% about the other person and only 20% or less about you? 20% is a maximum. Better if it's 100% about the other person. One tip is to go through your note and count how many times you wrote, "I." Then check that the "I" sentences quickly pivot to "you" or think about taking them out.

One big trap people fall into that makes a letter fail this test is when the note writer tries to relate their own experience to the experience of the note receiver. For example, maybe you had cancer, and you're writing to somebody that has cancer. The temptation is to write something like: *I've been through this also and here's my experience...*

This is not wrong per se, but self-relating will unintentionally diminish the recipient's unique and individual experience. Without realizing, you may be trumping their experience. Remember, the person you're writing to has a unique experience, and they want to be witnessed in their individual world. If you focus on what happened to you, you're changing the focus and as crazy as it sounds, you're actually diminishing the connection by relating yourself to their experience. If you must reference yourself, do so minimally perhaps making it a jumping off point to talk about them. Maybe this shows up as a suggestion that they're handling things in a way that you wish you had.

In Seattle, I worked with several high-profile professionals. In my dealings and conversations, I deliberately remained unassuming and discreet, never wasting their time talking about myself or my own good traits and successes. We instead focused on their goals, and I gave them honest, humble advice that never took into consideration what I personally might get out of the transaction. Before long, word spread that I was an honest, high-integrity realtor to work with. There's that fringe benefit again: more business came along when applying the philosophy.

When we went to look at a house, my clients were thinking about their children, pets, lifestyle in the space, and their lives. If I brought up my kids or my lifestyle, it would remove them from the magic of what they were trying to achieve—imagining themselves in this house. My job was to be as invisible as possible. That is your job while writing the note: to fade to the background and raise the other person up. Ironically, disappearing in this way will make the other person feel strongly that you are there for them. They'll perceive you as smarter and more of a leader than before. They'll feel more connected with you.

STEP 7: Reviewing what you wrote—is it 100% positive (unless it's an apology)?

When you stay curious about the world around you, you see life through the lens of positivity. This is your goal. *What matters to another person? What do you appreciate about that person? How do you make that person feel important?* Occasionally negative thoughts might sneak into the note. Look for them, cross them out, and start again.

> **Ask yourself, does this note contain anything that criticizes, condemns, or complains? If so, get rid of it.**

The only exception to this rule is when you're writing an apology note. Nobody's perfect, and certainly I've written my fair share of apology letters. It can feel pretty good for everyone involved to get an apology onto paper and out into the world. With these notes, the point is still to give the other person the stage, to acknowledge how you've impacted them, what their inconvenience was. Apology notes 2.0 (really great apology notes) also include how you plan to make it up to them. If you've made a mistake, you're humbling yourself, so in this instance talking a little in terms of yourself will be okay.

STEP 8: Reviewing what you wrote—is it honest and sincere?

This last step is the most important. You can't ever put enough emphasis on sincerity in your notes. An insincere note will not make a strong connection. *And it's hard.* This is why writing a good note takes so much thought.

You're going to run into some folks who are harder than others to write sincere, positive things about. For example, you might have a coworker who treats you poorly. Challenge yourself to stop and think about the person until you have something sincere and positive to write. If you can't write why you enjoy working with them, maybe say instead *I always enjoy walking by your desk and seeing all of your beautiful vacation pictures, you're really a jet-setter.* Or, *I admire how loyal you are to the company having worked here for 20 years.* Finding something true and positive to write makes a positive impact, and it also serves as a good reminder that when people are tough to work with, they're still humans who deserve kindness.

Interestingly, a few times when I've written these sorts of notes to people who have treated me poorly, people have responded with an apology. They all had their individual scenarios but treating them with kindness made them see they weren't on their best behavior much more clearly than a bitter reply to them would. One person explained to me how they were under a large amount of stress, and unwittingly did whatever it took to get through the day. I had given them grace and shown kindness and sincerity, and in return, they had returned that kindness and sincerity back to me.

STEP 9: Let it go

That's it. Send your note off into the world. You can post it on your kid's bathroom mirror, slip it into your husband's lunch bag, or stamp it and drop it in the mail. Sounds easy, right? But often, this last step can be surprisingly tough. We hold so much inside us and we're often so afraid to show our true selves. If you've done this right, then you're probably feeling a little vulnerable right now. This is completely normal. We've been trained our whole lives to be careful with how much of ourselves we let others see.

That's why the next chapter is about the feelings we have when we send a little piece of ourselves into the world. When we notice and validate these feelings, we've found the last key to the philosophy of note-writing. And only when we get past that, have we truly changed the way we are in the world.

My Dear General,

I do not remember that you and I ever met personally. I write this now as a grateful acknowledgment for the almost inestimable service you have done the country. I wish to say a word further. When you first reached the vicinity of Vicksburg, I thought you should do, what you finally did—march the troops across the neck, run the batteries with the transports, and thus go below; and I never had any faith, except a general hope that you knew better than I, that the Yazoo Pass expedition, and the like, could succeed. When you got below, and took Port-Gibson, Grand Gulf, and vicinity, I thought you should go down the river and join Gen. Banks; and when you turned Northward East of the Big Black, I feared it was a mistake. I now wish to make the personal acknowledgment that you were right, and I was wrong.

Yours very truly —A. Lincoln

Chapter Five

Sending Yourself into the World

On July 13, 1863, President Abraham Lincoln sent this remarkably honest and humble letter to General Ulysses S. Grant. In it, Lincoln personally admits that he had been wrong and Grant right concerning a piece of war strategy. Lincoln respectfully humbles himself by honoring Grant. What a concept—especially coming from a President of the United States. How often would you see such a letter written today? In fact, Abraham Lincoln sent many letters like this one in his career. But what I love most about Lincoln is that he didn't send letters like these to achieve some type of effect or to signal virtue, as we do in too many apologies today. He sent these letters because doing the right thing towards others was ingrained in his character. *Having high regard for others and doing the right thing will* bring the right *people* into your life so you can succeed faster and live a more meaningful life. It's not a coincidence that Lincoln is often ranked one of the greatest presidents in United State's history.

Compare this to our current world where we spend the majority of our time crafting an artificial online presence. We never think to admit mistakes, much less to sincerely apologize for them. More typically, we rationalize and/or feed our righteousness with stories that align with how others think or how we want others to see us in the world. By spending our time hitting the "like" button for things that make us feel good and scrolling past things we'd rather ignore, we protect our ego and fail to see other points of view. Meanwhile, we're unknowingly denying intimacy and creating distance, preventing opportunity for deeper relationships. Ultimately, we've become lonely and isolated. Intimacy requires understanding, humility, and truthful connections. Think about how Grant must have felt when he received this letter. How could it not have made him more loyal to his president and more deeply engaged in his resolve to perform well in the war?

But also think about how Lincoln must have felt writing this letter. After Lincoln's death, a law colleague of Lincoln's wrote, "It required no effort on his part to admit another man's superiority... that General Grant was right, and he was wrong about operations in Vicksburg." What he meant was that Lincoln was such a man of integrity, that it was second nature for him to write such a letter. But was it really no effort? I'd argue that even when you're the president of the United States of America, you make yourself vulnerable by admitting a mistake.

In fact, you make yourself vulnerable by showing up at all, whether you're apologizing or praising. That's why it's so tempting not to show up, but to lose ourselves in the digital world. No matter how you show up in the real world, it takes courage and some discomfort—courage that's hard to muster when it's so much easier to just hit "like" on someone's Facebook post and chase articles that feed preconceived views than to go beyond that to reach out with true intimacy and genuine thought. That Lincoln put himself out there wasn't easy, but he did it anyway. You can, too.

It's Not About You

Some people never send notes because they're too worried about whether the note sounds "okay." Your note doesn't need perfect grammar and it doesn't need perfect sentence structure. Put your insecurities aside in favor of thinking of the other person. The note is not about you. The goal is to think completely and wholeheartedly about what makes another person special, and then tell them that in your own words. Even if you're a little reluctant to send the note, why not send it anyway? What is there to lose? What is there to gain? I'm not saying this is easy. I get it. I've been there myself. What can be helpful is to view examples of notes that others have written to get your creative juices flowing which I provide in the latter part of this book. You'll see multiple examples of real notes people have written, notes that while not perfect in syntax or structure, were incredibly impactful for the recipient and often for the writer of the note as well.

Still, a lot of people struggle with the concept. *Just write notes? For no reason? When there's no birthday or anniversary?* Sometimes it's hard to get people beyond fixed thinking, beyond their self-doubt and hesitation, to throw away their myth of perfection, and to overcome the obstacles to reaching out. Remember, this is an exercise in deep thought about another individual. Just going through the exercise makes a difference. Sure, you can forego the note and instead tell the other person face to face what you think. And if you follow through, then excellent. You've understood the thought principle. But don't miss that sending hand-written notes lends tangibility and uniqueness in your connections with others. They can serve as mementos. They can be kept and revered, read and re-read, shared and witnessed by the recipient's acquaintances.

Getting Unstuck

If you're one of the people who just can't or won't do it, do not feel pressure to take a step you're not ready to take. Let's be honest, nobody responds well when others try to rah-rah them beyond readiness. Instead, give yourself the grace to accept where you are. Ask yourself: *what am I ready for? Where is a good place for me to start to be successful at this?* I'm going to offer a few suggestions to get you started wherever you are on the readiness scale. You can dip your toe into the water, climb down the ladder, or dive right in.

Write a note that you have no intention of sending. Then, crumble it up and throw it away.

When you write a note that you don't mean to send, it frees you to go deep. It allows you to say all the vulnerable things that you otherwise might not be able to, to experience the power of thinking deeply and honestly about another person without risking the vulnerability. So go back to chapter four, follow the ritual, and at the end, just crumble up that note and toss it.

Recently, I was telling a friend Lisa about note writing. She listened politely, but in her mind, she was thinking, *Yeah, okay, for you that works. But this isn't for me.*

A few weeks later, Lisa told me a story about a dinner party. The hostess wasn't a close friend, and an entire evening with this person was not something Lisa was looking forward to. She was worried they wouldn't be able to keep the conversation going, and that it was going to be an awkward evening. But then, Lisa remembered what I'd told her about writing notes as a way of deepening connections. She sat down, made her list of things she liked about the hostess, and then thought about stories about her hostess that demonstrated the good traits she saw in her. She even went so far as to write the hostess a note telling her how great she was. Then, Lisa threw the note away and went to the dinner party. Later, she told me about how much she enjoyed the process. She said, "Just the process of writing that note made me feel closer to my host. I felt more endeared to her, and she felt my newfound intimacy and mirrored it back to me. I know that it was that process of note writing that got me to that point and it somehow made the overall experience better."

Lisa had experienced that taking the time to sit down and think about another person let her understand them better. It opened her to the other person in ways she didn't expect. Even if the letter didn't go out, the mind-shift was real. She had deepened her relationship without sending the note. People don't realize that when they're worried about going out into the world—either literally by going to a dinner party or figuratively by sending a note—they are really thinking about themselves: how will they look, feel, act, and be judged? Note writing is about shifting the focus to the other person's world, making them feel seen and witnessed in a way that accentuates the good in who they are.

My favorite part of this story is that after the dinner party, my friend went back and actually wrote the host a thank-you note *and sent it*. Her note-writing career had begun.

Write a note to a person who doesn't (yet) exist

When my kids were babies, well before they could read, I started writing notes to their future selves. I wanted their adult selves to understand lessons that I learned the hard way. I wanted them to learn that achievement and happiness go hand-in-hand in the same way deep relationships and lifting other individuals up go hand-in-hand. Like the practice of writing notes that you never intend to send, writing notes to people who don't exist—in this case, to the future adult selves of children—puts you in the habit of sitting down and thinking deeply about others you care about, thinking about their futures and what you hope for them. It puts you in the habit of bringing yourself closer to those you care about and respect.

No kids? No problem. In fact, you probably have 1,000 less problems if you don't have kids and more time for note writing. Write notes to your future self, your past self, the friend or lover that you have or used to have, or someone you love who has passed away. The point is that you are focusing on someone else, going through the ritual, and practicing what it means to deepen your connections by getting out of your own head.

Write a note to someone you love deeply

I went upstairs yesterday and discovered that my eleven-year-old daughter had left a note pinned to my office door. It read, "Love you mom. Colette," and she drew a little basketball. It was 100% her personality. There certainly isn't much risk in leaving a note for a person she loved—me—but the effect was still powerful. When I saw it, I was excited. And when she got home, she was so pleased with herself, she ran into the house shouting, "Did you see it, Mom? Did you see my note?" So, I know that it brightened her day, too, with the expectation of the happiness it would bring me.

I have the same impulse as Colette. I'll leave my kids little surprise notes in their backpacks, lunch bags, and in their rooms. Sometimes they're for good luck and other times they're meaningless and silly. They create memories and lend a sense of importance that they won't feel with an impersonal text. It also keeps me in the habit of staying engaged with their world, and maybe for you, it's a good, safe place to start. Write your kids, your spouse, your mother, father, or your best friend.

Notice how you feel after writing the note. Maybe you were a little scared and nervous, outside your comfort zone at first. But maybe also, you discovered something about your feelings that opened you more to that person than you expected. Also, notice how they felt after they got your note, and how that deepened your connection even more. Are you now glad you sent it? Did they tuck the note away as a keepsake? Do you feel better about doing it again?

Write a note to a total stranger

Another thing you can do is write notes to famous people or total strangers. Does Adam Sandler really care that you admire him? Hate to break it to ya but probably not. But writing him a fan letter about how he inspired you to act might bring you back to a place of nostalgia and openness in a way just watching old YouTube clips wouldn't. Writing a note to a waiter at the restaurant or sending a note back complimenting the chef on a good meal isn't much of a risk, and yet you'll still experience the thrill of knowing how happy he might be even if just for a moment when he reads your hand-written words of praise.

Write a note for an occasion

Sometimes, it's easier to write notes for events of which notes are customary. There's a set format, and it doesn't feel as out of the ordinary. You can write birthday cards, thank you notes, or get-well-soon cards. When you do write inside pre-made cards, don't just write something trite. Do it the new way adding a line or two of personalized thoughts about the other person.

One inspiring example of how much going just a little bit beyond the usual can mean to a person happened when my dad landed in the hospital. He was supposed to be there four or five days, but he ended up being in there for sixty days. Things were looking bleak for a while, and my mom and I would make the hour drive to downtown Philadelphia every single day to visit.

Around day forty-five, he got COVID, and we could no longer visit him. Dad, being a social, outgoing person, took the isolation and loneliness hard. Before COVID, he was in a lot of pain, but he would get through it with a positive outlook by saying, *I just need to be there for my kids and grandkids. I need to watch them grow up.* But once COVID hit and he was isolated from people and connections, he lost his spirit. I began to hear things like, *I'm not doing well,* and I knew he'd gone to a mentally dark place. It wasn't the physical pain or injuries themself. In fact, he was recovering physically. It was the isolation. He missed and craved real human connection.

We could reach him with technology—video or voice calls, emails, and texts—in fact his phone was ringing off the hook with calls and texts, but somehow it wasn't the same. Kids that he used to coach in football, whom he hadn't talked to in years, were texting him. People sent flowers, meals and other little gifts. But still, he couldn't shake that feeling of loneliness.

When he arrived home from the hospital, he couldn't seem to shake his depression from being alone. Among all the flurry of good wishes that arrived, he got a letter from somebody from his high school whom he didn't even know that well, an acquaintance who had somehow gotten word that he was sick. She sent him a handwritten note. Not just a get-well card with a name scribbled on the bottom—he had lots of those—but a true, heart-felt letter with words of meaning.

Now, almost a year later, he's fine—completely recovered—and I have to tell you, he talks about this note almost every time I see him. It's almost as if it's all he can talk about after his whole hospital experience, and the after-hospital recovery, is this note and how he needs to write her a handwritten note back. He keeps on about that note to everyone. Whenever people come over, he pulls out the note. It's not because he knew about this book or because he knows how I feel about handwritten letters. The note hit him in a meaningful way that somebody had taken the time to sit down and write to him.

My father's not alone. I've seen it over and over in my own life. There's something about a text, email, or a quickly signed card that feels one way. But a handwritten note feels like, *Wow, somebody sat down and really thought about me.* Connection, true connection, is all about how you make someone feel. So, take the risk if you can. Reach out and try it. Put yourself out into the world in this small way, and I promise you, big things will happen.

Taking the Leap

The ritual of writing notes is an opportunity for you to think about other people and get your mind off yourself. It's not about the notes. It's not about the writing. It's about the philosophy behind the notes. Notes are one method of conveying to people, *I'm thinking about you, and I value you* in a way that's deeper and more purposeful than the split-second thought and anxiety inducing aftermath that goes with a quick text. Notes are a way of telling people that they matter by conveying their unique strengths and traits. Notes are a way of being in the world, of noticing the specialness of other people, the uniqueness of another's character. They speak to the importance of connection, positive sentiments, and seeing other people how they truly are. And they make your heart feel a little fuller knowing you've sent positivity out into the world.

You can get past your insecurities about note writing by starting small. You might be surprised at what you can do. I asked a friend of mine to read this book prior to publishing. Unbeknownst to me, this friend has a medical condition that causes his hands to shake. As a result, he's shied away from note writing, although always wanted to get back into it. This book inspired him to write a note anyway. Since he couldn't write legibly, he got creative and hid twelve word descriptions inside the card that he associated with who I am. Each word was printed and folded up on a small piece of paper. I was deeply touched. I thought about that note for weeks. I keep it near my desk at work to motivate me through the day and its officially become one of my favorite notes I've ever received. What made it so meaningful was not just the words he wrote, it was the fact that someone cared enough about me to set aside his own fears and insecurities to enrich my life. My regard for this friend went up 10 notches since receiving that note.

For more inspiration on how to get started, the next part of this book contains examples of actual notes and some of the stories behind them. As you read it, I hope it sparks ideas on how you can incorporate note writing into your own life.

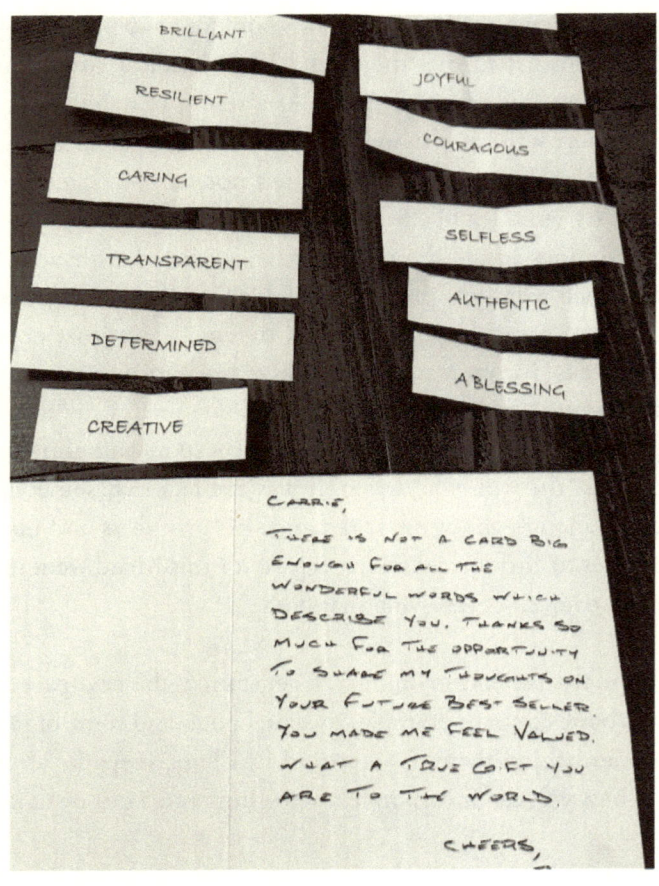

BRILLIANT

RESILIENT

JOYFUL

COURAGOUS

CARING

SELFLESS

TRANSPARENT

AUTHENTIC

DETERMINED

A BLESSING

CREATIVE

CARRIE,

THERE IS NOT A CARD BIG ENOUGH FOR ALL THE WONDERFUL WORDS WHICH DESCRIBE YOU. THANKS SO MUCH FOR THE OPPORTUNITY TO SHARE MY THOUGHTS ON YOUR FUTURE BEST SELLER. YOU MADE ME FEEL VALUED. WHAT A TRUE GIFT YOU ARE TO THE WORLD.

CHEERS,

Notes for Business

Incorporating this philosophy into your business model could not only bring more enjoyment to your role but it could also be incorporated as an effective strategy to reach business goals. A strong, dynamic business plan should include habits to ensure that those you aim to influence feel important. My business plan included a line-item for writing five handwritten cards a week. I bought notecards in bulk and made card writing part of my daily ritual. Think outside the box. Write a message on a post-it note when returning papers to someone's desk that lets them know they're appreciated. Or stick it on a photo you've really been admiring. You could write it on a plain, old piece of paper or even in the margins of a memo. Aside from the rule of appreciative thought, there are otherwise no rules. Let your creative juices flow, have fun and use your personality.

Remember "business" notes can be written to anyone—kids, teachers, family, friends, colleagues, strangers, famous people, and so on. While your notes don't have to go to business associates, writing notes to colleagues is a great way to build rapport and camaraderie within the office realm. It's a great way to gain their endorsement if you're seeking to influence them in some way. As a realtor, I would write notes to agents I worked with letting them know exactly what impressed me about working with them. Even though I wrote the notes with the intent of lifting another person up, you'd be surprised how far this simple act of note writing helped achieve my own business success: getting their endorsement in bidding wars, returning smoother transactions for my clients, and getting privileged information from friendlier agents who felt comfortable enough with me to share. The nice thing about handwritten notes in this day and age is they're so unexpected, people will be shocked you took the time. They will remember you more and hold you in higher esteem. And many will revel in the nostalgia.

In my first real estate brokerage, I worked with a successful real estate brokerage owner and realtor. To say he was a busy man was an understatement. One of the best pieces of real estate advice I had ever gotten was "never verbally negotiate." On the owner's birthday one year, I sent him a note saying how thankful I was for the day he was born, for not only did the world get a remarkable leader, but I got the best real estate advice I've ever received. I went on to say what a difference that advice made in my career and how fortunate I was to learn from such an experienced and intelligent negotiator like him. If you're curious if he appreciated that note, he not only loved the note, but kept the note at his desk permanently and read it out loud at his weekly meetings for the entire office to hear. I'll bet it made him feel on top of the world because how often do people get notes with such well thought out sentiments like that? Sadly, not often.

I was holding the brokerage owner in high esteem, but how do you think he regarded me? You bet our friendship and connection became timeless. Years later he acquired more businesses and I still know I can call him and he'll make time for me. This would never have happened if I'd sent him just another email or text. Digital media is simply not impactful in the same way as a handwritten note. I write notes of appreciation to everyone I work with. It creates relationships, connections, friendships—and business, too. And it makes me feel good going to bed each night knowing I've made another individual feel good.

When you think about business notes, think outside the box. Remember, these notes are not about you and they're not about business. Sure, they could potentially bring in business, but if they never do, you'll still get a personal lift from sending them. You'll know that they made someone feel great that day.

Occasionally, my business notes were sent on stationery with my real estate logo on them, but that was the only thing that expressed anything about real estate in the letter. I didn't mention I was a realtor and I never asked for business. I didn't even include my business card with it. People knew I was a realtor, because that's what the note paper said or because they knew me personally, but I never referenced my own personal business otherwise. This mindset earned me more business than I would have received if I droned on and on about what great realtors we were and how I would give them top service. The client wouldn't have cared all that much, they care infinitely more about how you view them then how they should view you. Once you understand this concept, your eyes will be opened to new business opportunities.

Writing notes is the type of thing people normally perceive as a waste of time concerning business. I would argue that this is one of the number one uses of your time.

As you read through the following sample notes, think about how each note would make you feel if you received it:

Dear Morgan,

Things have been busy with the holiday and the new job, but I wanted to make sure you knew that I see you crushing it out there. You are me, times ten. I see your efforts to grow and become better and better at what you do. I never stop counting my blessings in having met you. Thank you and keep up the good work.

Sincerely,
Carrie

Dear Alex,

I just wanted to drop a line to say a big thank you for offering such a great class to agents. I loved soaking in your innovative, bold spirit and big-picture thinking. Sharing listing knowledge is such a rare thing among agents. How generous of you to share yours—plus it's really the best advice out there as far as listings go.

In addition, you make it all so fun. Thank you again for a wonderful class, and I can't wait to start implementing your ideas and techniques in my business.

Sincerely,
Carrie

Dear Antwon,

Boy you really know how to make someone's whole day! Thank you so much for putting your confidence and trust in me by referring Scott Hall to me. I greatly appreciate it. I'll be sure to give him the top notch, 5-star, never-been-seen-or-given-before Carrie Pierce treatment!

Thank you again for thinking of me. It really means a lot.

Sincerely,
Carrie

Carrie,

Let me know when you get tired of being congratulated so much for being so awesome! Congrats on your 36th Ave closing.

Dave

Dear Shelly and Patrick,

Happy holidays to you guys! I still have that picture of Colette putting the moves on Elijah. She's no fool. She knows Elijah is a smartie and will probably invent something insanely genius when he's older. Miss you guys. Hope the house is treating you well.

Sincerely,
Carrie

Dear John and Brittany,

Congratulations on your beautiful new home! It was great to work with such genuinely nice people like you. I was so impressed with how hard you worked to win a home in such a competitive market. Great negotiating, Cliff! It's so rare to get a contingent offer accepted in this market, but your creative negotiating did it. Please don't hesitate to call should you need anything in the future.

Sincerely,
Carrie

The art of the business apology note:

Dear Marcus,

I'm counting my blessings this Thanksgiving and having been able to work with you is one of them.

I so love your penchant for excellence and how you always approach challenges as opportunities. Also, your candor is always appreciated. You have mastered timing and tone and have always stepped up to help me grow and learn when others weren't willing. Who better to deliver candor when it's needed than someone as down to earth as you? You have a knack for untangling a web of critical details to make quick and good decisions. I'm grateful for our time together. Have a great Thanksgiving.

Sincerely,
Carrie

Dear Kevin and Warren,

I just wanted to extend my sincere apologies for the way the end of your transaction went with Paul and Coldwell Banker. I understand the inconvenience it caused. The lack of service detail provided to you was inexcusable. I hope you'll accept this gift as my way of trying to make up for it a little, and I know Tanya's high standards of service should make for a better experience on the sale of your townhome.

Sincerely,
Carrie

I'll bet there's not one person in the world who hasn't made a mistake or done something to negatively impact another. How would it make the other person feel to get a note like the one above from someone who made a mistake? Did I feel uncomfortable writing it? Sure, I did. But the note wasn't about me. It was about acknowledging the other person and making them feel as if they mattered. No promises here, but I'd be willing to bet that a good letter may even impress the other person in a situation where they initially could have harbored a lot of anger or resentment So when you're thinking about writing business notes, do like Lincoln did and think deeply about the other person, be willing to admit your mistakes, and express sincere regret at how you've hurt or inconvenienced the other person.

So—your turn. Try it. Put note writing in your business plan and see what happens. Then, write me a note and let me know how it went.

Tips for Business Notes:

Think outside the box.

- Remember, notes are not about you and they're not about business. They are 100% about the other person.
- Apology notes are an honorable way to deal with mistakes. It will strengthen connections where you otherwise might lose one.

Chapter Seven

Kids and Note Writing

A new comic themed restaurant opened in our town right before the COVID-19 pandemic. It was a terribly difficult time as we saw restaurant after restaurant going out of business. One trip to this new restaurant and we knew it would be our future favorite spot. The food was delicious, service down to earth and friendly, vibe was fun. That would be enough to do us in, but even the menu items were clever. The fish and chips were called "I Found Nemo." When the world cautiously began to re-open, we went back to this restaurant as often as we could. Because we loved it and because we're in the habit of thinking of others, we thought of ways to keep them encouraged during the challenging times. My daughter Piper wrote them this very cute letter:

> Thank you for giving me a very good time and a good dinner you are my favorite restorant and I hope you have enough money to stay. I am telling everyone about the Pop Inn. Thank you

I can't be entirely sure if it was the note that did it, admittedly we're also good tippers, but to this day the restaurant treats us a little like royalty. Maybe it was the thought and appreciation that goes along with writing notes, or maybe it was the note itself, or perhaps a little of both, but they've told us we're one of their favorite customers. They even gave my Dad a free hat when he was in the hospital. My daughter didn't write the note to get this type of treatment. She did it to uplift someone she cared about. The bonus wasn't the free stuff and royal treatment. It was getting a deeper connection with the owners. This is not just a book on note writing, this is a different way of living your life. Taking the time to think about another human being is a lost art that we need to bring back. It's a shift in focus from yourself and your online personas to more authentic relationships and heartfelt consideration of others. We need to bring this back and kids being our future are a promising start.

Teaching kids to write notes the way I describe in this book helps them see new ways to make a difference in their lives and other people's. I say "new" because for the upcoming generations, this is a new concept. It's unfortunate that texting and e-messaging will be their norm, but the good news is adopting the age-old practice of handwritten notes can be a way for them to differentiate themselves, to separate themselves from the pack. Note writing also shows kids how it feels to make other people happy, and teaches them that true connections mean thinking of another human being in a better way than technology could ever offer. Don't let them miss the good in the old ways of doing things. Don't let them forget how important the exercise of deep consideration of others can be in relationships. Help them understand that while technology is quick, convenient, and sometimes necessary, it lacks the warmth and sincerity that good old-fashioned handwritten notes can bring.

The other side of the coin is the importance of writing notes *to* our kids. Getting kids to write notes starts with writing notes to kids. I have lists about what I love about my kids, the personality traits that makes them uniquely themselves. These are my "cheat sheets" but they are incredibly helpful when I want to make my kids feel special. This is especially important for my 10-year-old twins, to make sure they feel independent and separate from each other. When I write them notes, I'll draw from the lists and let my thoughts about them flow. Recently, one of my daughters graduated from elementary school, so I went to the list and wrote her a note telling her what makes her amazing in my eyes:

Dear Colette,

Congratulations! Boy am I proud of you. I wish you could see yourself through my eyes. I see how you rise to challenges, always trying your best. And you go the extra yard with extra credit and your studying, something I love to see. You're a real born leader, fearless, ambitious, yet kind and generous. That's a hard combination to come by and it will serve you well throughout your life. I love you to pieces. Onward with your promising journey into middle school.

Love,
Mom.

Bob Goff, author of *Love Does*, says that when you tell someone who they are, they will become it. If you tell kids they are something, they'll become it whether that something is good or bad. Parents who tell their kids they're bad will watch their kids become just that. Parents who tell their kids they're good will watch them thrive. If you tell them in a hand-written note, they'll be able to refer back to your words and read them again and again. The impact you can make on kids is magical.

I'll give an example of Bob Goff's philosophy in action using notes. My oldest daughter frequently fights with her twin sisters. Ever since her twin sisters were born, it's been hard for the oldest to find her own space. She has such a big heart. I've seen it at work. But she doesn't always show it and when she doesn't get enough attention, she instead picks fights with them. To reinforce good behavior, I wrote her a note telling her who she is:

> Colette, I know how much you love your sisters. You have such a big heart. It's one of your best qualities.

Notice I didn't write negative things or bad behavior references. It's calling out her best in a way that helps her find the courage to express it in the world. It gives her the confidence to choose the good in herself.

A friend of mine had a similar situation, she told me about a note she found from her older daughter written out to her younger sister:

> I have a secret. I hate when you leave me out. You don't know what it feels like. It's such a pain in the

butt and lonely. It's like you're at the buddy bench, and no one asks you, Do you want to play, but even worse. I love you much. No matter what. Hope you have a good night sleep. I love you.

Then she drew a picture of them holding hands with a heart around it. My friend mentioned that her daughter is usually not expressive, but notes offered her daughter a way to express herself. They brought forth her loving side. For kids, the act of writing notes in this way can be therapeutic. They want to share their feelings and it's difficult to do this using an app where their focus gets riddled by distraction after distraction, inherently the reality of internet and iphone use. Even at a young age, people crave deeper connections and they cannot exercise the meaningful thought required for this goal without distraction-free space to do so.

We can't talk about notes and kids without pointing out how much people love getting notes from kids. Encourage your kids to send notes to all the important people in their lives. A teacher told me that she's been saving notes from her students for over twenty years. When she needs a little uplift, she goes to her file:

> The most memorable [note] was from a former 8th grade student when she graduated high school. In her note she told me she would not have graduated if it had not been for me. That it was my compassion and support that helped her stay motivated in school (even though I did not talk to her after she left middle school). She added that it was because of me that she was going to college to become a teacher. It was the best compliment and one of the best moments of my career! Yes, notes do matter and they keep me going in tough times. Very impactful!

A mother I know keeps a note from her daughter that simply says: *"Dear Mom, I love you! Meet me on the couch. Love T."* I love that such a seemingly ordinary note was still special enough to save as a keepsake. This would not have the same effect if it were a text.

Another person I know used to leave messages in her daughter's lunchbox. According to her, "It was simple things like, 'you are my pumpkin' or 'have an awesome day.'" At some point [my daughter] hit an age when she was embarrassed by them, and I stopped. Then one day when she was almost an adult, she made a lunch box for me to take to my work with a note from her. That was sooo sweet." These same notes could never carry the same depth of meaning if they were sent by text, email, or social media.

An important type of note your kids should learn to write is the apology note. They'll make a lot of mistakes in life—we all do. Apologizing by note is a great way to show kids that mistakes aren't the end of the world, and it doesn't have to mean the end of relationships. In fact, if the note is done right, it can strengthen relationships because let's be honest, nobody's Mother Theresa, we all make mistakes. What makes good character is how you respond to your own mistakes. Instruct kids that within their note they should acknowledge the inconvenience caused to the other person and how they plan to make it up to them.

A few years ago, I was teaching my oldest daughter about the importance of self-responsibility and respecting others. She was told to never complain to the referee. It's disrespectful and it deflects focus from her own responsibility. My daughter was in a heated basketball game one day when the referee called a foul. Now between you and me it probably wasn't a foul but that matters absolutely zero in my book, the rule is no complaints. Well, she broke the rule and threw her hands up in protest at the ref's foul call. Then she looked at me in the crowd with a guilty look like she knew she'd done wrong. Take a wild guess what the consequence was for her actions. You guessed it, she had to write an apology note to the referee. This is what she wrote:

Dear Ref:

I'm sorry I had a bad attitude and threw my hands up at you in the game. I genuinely would start that all over. Thanks for helping me learn.

As you might guess, the referee got a big kick out of it. He showed it to his whole referee crew and later told us that it had made his day. Referees get beat up game after game, how nice is it for them to come across this type of kindness? How often do you think a referee gets a note like that? How do you think the difference in feeling and meaning would have been if she sent a text message instead of a hand-written note? Another benefit besides giving a lift to the referee's day was that the lesson to my daughter really hit home. She didn't complain the rest of the season. She stopped thinking of herself and thought instead of the refs, making her a better person and a better player every time she stepped onto the court. And it also narrowed her game focus on being a better player instead of shifting blame. We saw that referee in games multiple times after that, and as an unintended bonus, we noticed him giving my daughter small words of encouragement and teaching a little more as he made calls in the game. How cool is that?

The final and maybe best reason to engage your kids in note writing is that later, when they're all grown up, you'll have their notes with all their handwriting and personality. Those notes will become priceless to you.

The other day, my mother told me that she had recently read a handwritten welcome book on her vacation, and the handwriting looked eerily like her own mother's. She couldn't seem to get it out of her mind. She was drawn back again and again to look at that manual during the vacation. Someone else told me about his Mom's calligraphy and how he keeps a calligraphic note written to his son as a keepsake and a reminder to carry on the tradition of practicing calligraphy. Handwriting is such a beautiful representation of personality. As we swiftly move through our technological evolution, I hope we never lose the fine art of handwriting. I know we'll never lose our emotional connection to it.

Tips for notes to and from kids:

- Kids don't forget your core values if you put them into notes. In my notes to my kids, I always remind them, *this is who you are. You know you're this. I know you're this. This is what makes you so great.* When writing notes to your kids who are going through challenges, call out their best traits and remind them of their core values.
- Don't wait for special occasions to write your kids notes. Make a "cheat sheet" like I do, a list of their great traits and then find examples of them showing up with those traits. Every time they do, write them a note.
- Encourage your kids to focus on seeing things from the other person's point of view.

Chapter Eight

Notes to Strangers

A good friend of mine recently lost her father to cancer.
She went to get her mail one day and noticed a card from
someone unexpected—her mailman. He had heard about
her father's death through the grapevine and felt moved to
express his sympathy. His card was written with exactly the
touch of thoughtful sincerity I preach in this book. My
friend received a lot of cards from family and friends after
her father's death, but this note from her mailman touched
her more than any of the other cards she received. To her,
the impact of the note was a little more distinct and touch-
ing *because* it was sent by a stranger.

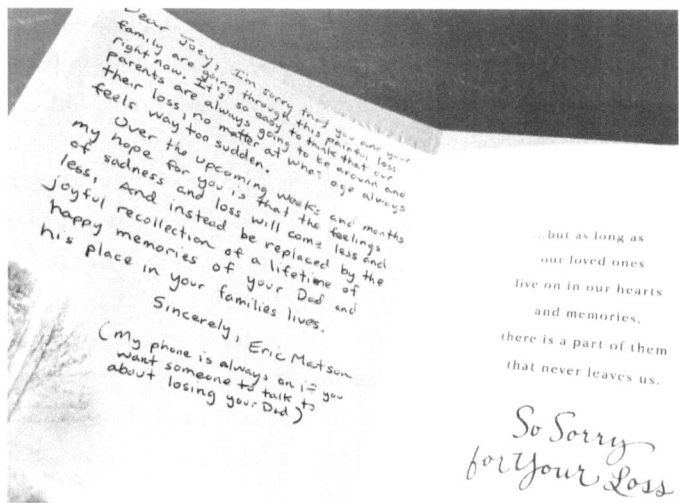

Writing cards to strangers is not an easy task. The default mode with those we don't know is to withdraw, to err on the side of caution, to be worried about how the recipient might feel getting a card from someone they hardly know. Why would you put yourself on the line, and be vulnerable to a stranger? I say why not? What do you have to lose?

Witnessing the lives of others and lending support is a gift that you can give anyone. If genuinely expressed in a way that acknowledges another, the note will always land in a positive and sometimes powerful way. Stop worrying about what people will think of you or you'll be robbing them of a message they might be craving to hear. Instead, think of how you will make others feel and how you can brighten the life of the other person. When people feel really seen, when their problems and inconveniences are truly witnessed by another, then life becomes more tolerable for that person.

A few years back when I lived in Washington state, I did a major remodel and second story addition on my house. Construction vehicles were going to be parked in the neighborhood from early morning until dinnertime for a minimum of three to six months. I dreaded the noise and the eyesore of the construction vehicles and how it would disrupt my neighbors. Knowing what an inconvenience I was causing my neighbors, I wrote each house on my street a personalized note. In the note, I told them how much I appreciated them as neighbors. I apologized in advance for the inconvenience of the construction. I told them that I understood the construction vehicles could frequently be in their way and that the noise would be an unpleasant thing they'd have to put up with. I asked them to contact me personally if they needed anything or had any questions. For the neighbors directly on each side of me, I also included a bottle of wine for their troubles.

Later, I had several neighbors tell me how lucky they felt to live in such a warm neighborhood. One even told me that the person who lived there before me never spoke a word to them in the twenty years they had lived next to them. This experience that had the potential of polarizing me from my neighbors brought us closer together. Several asked to stop by and see the progress, and we landed in a closer relationship position than we had before construction. And I'm proud to say we didn't have a single issue or complaint from any of our neighbors in the six months it took to complete the project.

There are so many opportunities to write to people you hardly know.

If you can't think of someone to write a card to, then maybe you're not thinking hard enough. The possibilities are endless. I've written to the head of Homeowners Associations to thank them for doing such a thankless job. I've written cards to my daughters' school counselors, teachers, and coaches. During COVID, I offered my full support and told them that I recognized how difficult their job was and also that they have the endless admiration from our family because there was no precedent for what they were having to deal with. I wrote a note to our office IT guy when he was going through a rough time with his health.

I've written many notes to my dad's doctors. During dad's 60-day hospital stint he had one night nurse who was particularly good to him to the point where dad, heavy on drugs at this point, kept urging me to give that nurse a wad of cash for the extra good service. While I didn't oblige to the wad of cash, I did send the nurse a note of appreciation. I truly wanted to elevate the nurse and let him know that his hard work and extra tender care with my dad was seen and mattered to not only my dad but to our whole family.

The above examples give you some ideas, but I'll offer you some others. Have you ever had someone give you a piece of advice that you never forgot? Why not write that person a note to share how much that meant to you? Have you ever received over-the-top service from someone? Write them a note—or even better, write a note to their manager telling the manager how impressed you were. Has a neighbor raised polite kids? Write them a note telling them so. What about that first job you landed and the boss who took a chance on you? Write the company owner a note to tell them how much you appreciated that and what you learned from working for them. Are you starting to get your own ideas of who to write notes to?

About four years ago, my oldest daughter and I flew to San Francisco. Because I'm always looking for opportunities to write cards, I keep spare notes in my purse. While waiting to board the plane my daughter and I decided to write thank you notes to each of the Alaska Airlines flight attendants thanking them for all they do. In the note, we acknowledged that they probably have to put up with a lot of ungrateful and disrespectful people while still maintaining a smile and looking out for other's safety and best interests. I noted how their reassuring smiles and hellos while onboarding the plane never went unnoticed by me because it always calmed my nerves and gave me the sense that all will be okay. To put an exclamation to the gesture of gratitude, I grabbed a $5 Starbucks gift card at the airport and included it with the note. Well, let me tell you, I've never received such reception on a flight. Although I didn't expect it or do the gesture for this purpose, my daughter and I got the royal treatment, including free entertainment tablets, frequent personal check ins, and all sorts of extra goodies. We were checked on so often we felt spoiled. But the greater gift was the uplifting feeling I got from those flight attendants being happier.

When my mother was a kid, she loved Lay's brand potato chips so much that she wrote a note to the Lay's company telling them how their potato chips were her absolute favorite. A few weeks later, she came home to a large package on her doorstep from Lay's. They thanked her for her enthusiasm for their company and included bags and bags of Lay's brand snacks for her to enjoy. What a great time in our history that we could simply write a handwritten note to a company and have them respond back in a way that was so personal.

Unfortunately, in today's world, this type of exchange is going extinct. The speed of exchange and mass automated responses have replaced personalized communication. Companies do everything they can to deflect from depersonalized communication, requiring you to email them or talk to a virtual robot instead. It's becoming a lucky thing to get an actual person beyond an online chat. How great would it be, to run into a company where old-fashioned human beings answered the phone, without the headache of a phone tree, was the norm? Some of these companies require James Bond-like craftiness to get to a real person. It's dehumanizing and impersonal but it's also an opportunity for businesses to set themselves apart. As unrealistic as it might sound, a company where humans pick up directly, and thoughtful handwritten notes are the norm, that would be a company I could get loyal with. I'd pay extra for that. I wonder how many company lawsuits could be avoided with this type of personal interaction. I've seen touches of this on websites like Etsy and Poshmark where small businesses care enough to add the extra touch of a handwritten note. When I get them, I like that business a little more because they took the time to write the note.

Getting back to writing notes *to* companies, if you do your homework and get a little creative, there are still ways to get handwritten notes seen by people at companies and you can bet they'll be viewed as unique and appealing. The more personalized the card, the more effective it will become. It's important to note that this shouldn't be done in order to receive something in return. It should be done with the intent of making another person's world a little better, making them feel like they matter. To get a company's address, you can call the company, google the company headquarters, or ask that online chat person at what address they receive "snail mail."

Tips for notes to and from strangers

Every stranger has a name and taking the time to learn it can change their whole day. Many service workers wear name tags or introduce themselves. Next time you're in a situation when that happens, make focused listening a habit and try to remember the person's name. Even jot it down on paper or into your phone. Even if you don't have the courage yet to send a note to that person, just watching the effect of using that person's name in your exchanges is a great first step to understanding how feeling seen can affect a stranger on a deeper level.

- Keeping your notes to strangers anonymous is a great way to get started with experiencing the power of the handwritten note. Carry some notepaper, envelopes, and a pen with you, and commit yourself to slipping one note a week to a stranger you encounter. Tell them how much you love their smile, or how you recognize how hard their job is and how you appreciate their presence. Notice how it makes you feel after you put it out into the world. Notice how it makes you feel the next time you encounter that person. If you get the sense the note could come across as creepy, add a PS and tell them about this book and how it inspired you to write the note to them.
- Writing notes to companies instead of individual people is another good way to get started with experiencing the power of notes. Did someone provide great service? Why not put that in writing to their head of customer service? A lot of people write notes when they're unhappy with service, so imagine the effect of the positive note.
- With notes to strangers—as for all notes—think in terms of abundant application. Instead of acting on the side of caution and restraint, act out of extreme love and joy. You want to always be cognizant of how lonely and disconnected our world is, and how every drop of kindness you show can be the difference that someone needs to get through their day.

Conclusion

We are so distracted—clicking, scrolling, texting, jump-ing from one screen to the next. It separates us from the real world, making us feel lonely and disconnected. Fill your cup and live a more joyful life by taking the time to think about what makes other people great, and then tell them in a handwritten note.

As you go through your day, notice the people who you interact with and what you appreciate about them. Challenge yourself to leave your phone alone and instead think about the grocery store clerk while you stand in the grocery line, the woman in charge of pick-up at your kid's daycare, or the colleague you're emailing back and forth at work. Challenge yourself to think about your siblings, cousins, nieces, nephews. Don't forget your own kids and your spouse—also your mom and dad and best friends. There are a million opportunities around you to really see and acknowledge the people in your world. But you need to stop clicking and stop texting to really take notice.

When you stay curious about the people around you, everyone's life improves. Take notice of the way a person cares for a child who's having a really hard time or a stranger who opens the door for an elderly person. Anytime you think, *wow, that's nice,* you've found potential material for a card.

Note writing is a mindset of gratitude. It keeps you positive. It keeps you connected. It keeps you creative and keeps you sharp. It's a way of living that offers greater abundance and joy. Why not go about your day joyful, knowing that you have the power to lift others? Leave a little note on a tip: *You're the best waiter. I love your sweater. Compliments to the chef.* It's so small, and yet you might have made someone's day, even their entire week. That person might have taken that note home to put on their fridge forever. It'll make you feel great. And make them feel great. This is the mindset of abundance and joy.

Note writing changes your whole attitude. Dale Carnegie told us to smile when you're with others. Now, when you're by yourself, take the time to focus on another person and write notes. When you do this, you're paying attention to what's important to the other person. To what really matters to them. You're slowing your world down. When you send that note, you've sent that smile into the greater world.

In that sense, this book is not about writing notes. It's about a way of being in the world. It's about how your soul connects with another soul. It's about deepening connections. It's about deepening relationships. It's about getting your heart closer to someone else's. It's about lifting one another up and lending a helping hand in a sincere way. It's about developing a habit through note writing of connecting with the world. Through writing notes, you have learned how to be in the world.

Now, when you put down your pen and paper and go out into the world, that spirit of abundance, joy, and connection carries over into everything you do. As always, Dale Carnegie puts it best when he says that the power of appreciation is one of our most valuable tools, and that one of the most important habits in life is when you experience true gratitude, you must express it.

This book, for me, is the longest note I've ever written. Me, to you. I am grateful for you. I appreciate that you read this book to the end. I appreciate your curiosity and hunger for self-growth. Did you know that curiosity, hunger and other-thinking also happen to be the top traits seen in great leaders? Reading this book shows the potential you have to do great things. Internalizing these principles will make you a great human and leader. I see in you a desire to connect with the world and I see in you the great joy that is possible in your life. I know that you've got this. I know you can do it. I know that before you lies a richer, more connected life.

Couldn't the world use more notes right now?

(Signed, Carrie Pierce)

Love

LOVE LETTER

Dear T-

Hello gorgeous. Happy 20th birthday! I'm happy that I can be here with you today and thankful that we get to spend this time together. Celebrating you is so easy to do. I'm so proud of you. You are an intelligent beautiful and absolutely hilarious person and I'm grateful to have that and you in my life. I know you would rather stay a teen forever, but entering your twenties only means that we are getting closer to spending our 30s, 40s and 50s, and beyond together. It's exciting. I can't wait for more birthdays to celebrate with you and I hope that with this one, you recognize all of the accomplishments you have achieved with all of your incredible talents! It's encouraging (in a good way) to think back to our birthday last year and reflect on everything you've done (that makes me happy) and you've done A LOT! I'm proud and I love the person you are unconditionally. You are the love of my life. Happy 20th Birthday, lovie!

Love,
H-

P.S- I love you

LOVE LETTER

Dear K-

We've only been together a short amount of time but in that time, you've become my world. You are one of a kind. I've never in my life been cared for and understood as well as I feel with you. You are intelligent and deep in the way that you care, and you make me a better person just for being around you. What we have together is beautiful. You make me feel so incredibly special and happy. I never want to let you go. Every time I look at your handsome face, I think how did I get so lucky? Everything about you is irresistible. There's a future together for us, and it may have its ups and downs but it will also be beautiful. I want everything for you and to be everything to you. You have my heart.

XOXO-
D-

Love Letter

Dear B-

Happy First Wedding Anniversary! Baby I cannot tell you how many ways you have made me a better and happier person. It still brings anxiousness to my stomach every time you look at me. If feels like we have been together for so long; yet you affect me like we are still sooo new. While I never wish our lives away I cannot wait for the next 50 years to unfold and to realize all of the adventures we will have together. I will never let my love for you fade because the time we have been together increases. I will make a promise to you here, on our first anniversary: I will love you and show my love for you as strong as I have shown my love for you this past year each and every year of the rest of our lives.

Love you baby with all of my heart.
N-

Love Letter from Johnny Cash to June Carter Cash

Happy Birthday Princess

We get old and get used to each other. We think alike. We read each other's minds. We know what the other one wants without asking. Sometimes we irritate each other a little bit. Maybe sometimes take each other for granted. But once in a while, like today, I meditate on it and realize how lucky I am to share my life with the greatest woman I ever met. You still fascinate and inspire me. You influence me for the better. You're the object of my desire, the #1 earthly reason for my existence. I love you very much.

John

My Darling Wife

This note is to warn you of a diabolical plot
entered into by some of our so called friends —
(ha!) calendar makers and even our own children.
These and others would have you believe we've
been married 20 years. 20 minutes maybe —
but never 20 years. In the first place it is a known
fact that a human cannot sustain the high level of
happiness I feel for more than a few minutes —
and my happiness keeps increasing.
I will confess to one puzzlement but I'm sure it is
just some trick perpetrated by our friends — (Ha
again!) I can't remember ever being without you
and I know I was born more than 20 mins ago.Oh
well — that isn't important. The important thing
is I don't want to be without you for the next 20
years, or 40, or however many there are. I've gotten very used to being happy and I love you very
much indeed.

Your Husband of 20 something or other.
Ron

BIRTHDAY

Dear S-

So proud to have a cousin of your caliber. I find myself bragging about you often and then when I show people your picture they say "Oh she's beautiful too!" And I say "heck yeah she is!" I hope you have a great birthday.

Love
D-

LETTER FROM A CHILD TO A SOLDIER

Dear Soldier

Thank you for your bravery and for keeping us all safe. My name is T- and I live in Clinton, NJ. I have a dog and 2 cats and I have a wonderful family and I am so thankful that we are all safe because of you. Thank you so much and good luck!

Love,
T-

Thank You

Dear D-

I can't thank you enough for your efforts in organizing the meal train and the delicious dinner that you provided. I know that I'm very lucky to have such caring and thoughtful friends during my recovery journey. I appreciate all you did and will be forever grateful for your kindness.

J-

Dear K-

Thank you for making my weekend so special.
It was everything I could hope for, my kids and
their kids together. If I could have one wish come
true, I would wish that all moms could have a
daughter like you. You have been a rock for me
this last year. I love all the gifts, but the best gift
is one you've already given me. You're moving
out here, and little spontaneous visits are the
things that brighten my day every day. There
aren't words sufficient enough to show how
much I love you.

All my Love,
M-

Dear P-,

Thank you so much on having Brandon + Preston for a day. I did not expect such fun and creative activities. You probably didn't know this, but you saved me a little that day too because I had a lot of work to get done. Thank you again so much for being so engaged with the girls + helping me out!

Sincerely,

Dear S-,

Just wanted to drop a line to say thank you for talking me through your experience with Haley. Your husband always talks about all the incredible things you do as a mom. When we hung up, I thought, "Wow I think I just witnessed what he was talking about." Haley is so lucky to have such a dedicated Mom and I'm lucky to have your wisdom. Thank you for the time you spent on our call.

Sincerely,
C

Dear S-,

Thanks for keeping an open mind as well as open door where needed. Your drive and dedication inspire me. Plus you are so fun and enthusiastic. Onward to accomplish great things with you.

K-

Dear K-

Thank you for the exceptional job you've done.
I also want to thank you for taking care of me
while I was sick. No one would have done so
much to help care for another person than you.
Your future is so bright. Enjoy your time off, you
deserve it.

G-

Business

Dear H-,

You worked so hard to give us a wonderful first home buying experience! Thank you for everything, for answering all our questions, walking us through the process and dealing with all our crazy issues! You were tireless, fierce, and simply amazing.

Thanks
(K-, J-, R-, & A-)

Dear D-,

Just wanted to drop a note to once again to con-
gratulate you on your very special home. It was
truly a pleasure to work with you and if you
don't mind me saying, I think you're quite a brilliant person. You were a pro at studying people's
motives and calmly figuring out the right way to
handle difficult situations and I also noticed how
good you were at study details closely while still
not getting too wrapped up in it to miss the big
picture goal. On many different occasions I saw
you make tough decisions easily and with grace.
I think these are really great, unique qualities. I
feel really lucky to have worked with you and it's
really no wonder your company fought so hard to
hire you. Congrats again! Please don't hesitate to
call if you need anything.

Sincerely,
C

Dear K-,

Just sitting here thanking my lucky stars for you, you're a total gift of an assistant. You are the most perfect you there is. And you are the reason I can enjoy time with my family while still serving my clients as exceptionally well as I like to do. For that I thank you.

XOXO,
C

Dear C,

Thank you so much for all your help and hard work over the past few months! You have helped us find and move into our dream home! We are so excited and grateful. Wishing you and your loved ones continued health.

Sincerely,
G and C-

Dear M-,

It was so great connecting with you and understanding more about your goals. Your intuition
is impressive and your energy level through
the roof. No doubt these traits have led to the
high success you've already experienced in your
career. I'm looking forward to seeing all the great
things ahead for you.

Sincerely,
C-

Dear L-,

Just wanted to send a quick note to say thank you for another job well done on the Chen transaction. It's nice to have so much experience and wisdom guide a transaction especially when challenges come up like they did with ours. You handled them expertly. Look forward to our next one together.

Sincerely,
C-

Dear A-,

Just wanted to drop a note to say thank you for all the great work you and your team have been doing on my transactions. It seems like they've all had their unique challenges, yet you were a rock through everyone. And it's so appreciated during this busy season. I know I never have to worry about a thing when transactions are in your hands.

Sincerely,
C-

Dear T-,

I wrote this card for the sole purpose of telling
you how gifted you are, and I think you should go
after that opportunity you were telling me about.
Your talents are multi-faceted, and if I'm judging
by what I've seen you accomplish in the past, you
have what it takes. You're really an inspiration
and it's fun to hear about all of your successes.
Keep me posted on what happens.

Sincerely,
C-

Dear S-,

One Monday night I saw a young child acciden-
tally go into the pool and struggle, she was very
upset. It was a scary moment. What you did then
as her instructor was brilliant and carried so
much wisdom. You didn't panic or react in a way
to upset the child further, with a really calm and
caring composure you asked the child to jump
right back in the pool again. This calmed the
child and her parents down because they knew
everything was ok and having the child jump
right back in reversed any fear she might have
carried with her that night. I just wanted to say
how impressed I was with the way you handled
the situation. You're clearly a pro.

Sincerely,
C-

Special Occasion

Dear S-,

Happy Birthday to someone I have so much respect for. You are my friend that cuts down trees and hauls them down a hill in freezing cold, stormy weather. You single mom it with all the heart in the world for your boys. And you do your work with honesty and integrity. You are one of a kind, I mean it, they don't make 'em like you anymore. I love ya and miss you.

Love,
C-

Dear C and F-,

Happy Holidays and best wishes to one of the most entrepreneurial families I know. I continue to sit back and just admire all that you do.

Cheers!
C-

Dear Y-,

Happy Belated Birthday to my fun, fab, fearless friend! You are the kind of person I wish I was friends with my whole life. I feel like 30 years of my life just got jipped. You're a very special person. The world would be a better place if more people were just like you.

Sincerely,
C-

Dear N-,

Congratulations on your upcoming addition
to the family. You must be overjoyed. I love the
name you picked for your oldest Divya and I'll bet
you'll have fun deciding on her baby brother or
baby sister's name. You do parenthood with such
grace and make it look easy. That little one is in
good hands with you.

Sincerely,
C-

Dear S-,

Keep kicking cancer's a⁓*. You got this. Your kids have no idea what a strong mom they have. But they will. Praying for you.

Love & Soft Hugs,
C-

Dear J-,

Congratulations on your new digs! You should
be proud of yourself. Buying a home these days
should come with a trophy. It's so hard and you
did it with incredible amounts of determination
and hard work. I frequently found myself standing in awe, nice work girl.

C-

Apology

Dear M-,

Just wanted to send a note to say how sorry I
am for the communication error last week. This
business is hard enough without having to deal
with what happened. It must have been a terrible
night for you to wait like that and then explain
to the sellers that you had no answers when they
were promised an answer. I want you to show
this note to the sellers so they know the fault was
with me. I take full responsibility. If I can make a
call personally to your client, please let me know.

Sincerely,
C-

Dear P-

I'm writing this to apologize for not including you in my wedding party. The decision was difficult with so many family members I had to consider. And you've meant the world to me, of my friends you have always been one of my best supporters and my closest confidantes. It just seems wrong not to have you as bridesmaid, indeed I feel terrible about it. If you'll allow me to, I'd like to make it up to you when I return from the honeymoon. Would you let me take you out for a nice dinner? Please let me know, I'm grateful for our friendship and you are a very important person in my life.

Love,
E-

Dear M-,

I want to apologize for arriving 15 minutes late to our appointment on Saturday. It was very unprofessional on my part and I know it caused you an inconvenience. You are busy with work and family, and an additional 15 minutes might have given you time to accomplish a lot more than waiting for me to arrive. I usually make sure I call in advance when I'm late but the lack of cell service prevented me from doing so. However, there are no good excuses for this and I am indeed very sorry for the trouble. I may not have shown it on Saturday but your time is very valuable to me. I want to assure you it will not happen again.

Please let me know if I can do anything else to help you. We have another meeting next weekend and I plan to show 30 min to all future meetings so this never happens again. I look forward to seeing you then.

Sincerely,
T-

Letter from Barack Obama to
an Art History Teacher

Ann,

Let me apologize for my off-the-cuff remarks. I was making a point about the jobs market, not the value of art history. As it so happens, art history was one of my favorite subjects in high school, and it has helped me take in a great deal of joy in my life that I might otherwise have missed.

So please pass on my apology for the glib remark to the entire department, and understand that I was trying to encourage young people who may not be predisposed to a four year college experience to be open to technical training that can lead them to an honorable career.

Sincerely,
Barack Obama

Worksheet for Thinking About Others

for The Purpose of Note Writing

Person's Name

What do I appreciate about them?
Why do they matter to me?
Why do they matter to others?
What is it that makes them special and unique?

Write your note rough draft focusing more on "you" than "I" statements. Keep it short and sweet. About 4-8 sentences is a good rule of thumb.

Now pick a notecard, stationery or whatever you plan to use, hand write a final draft and deliver the note.

To download printable copies of this worksheet, and for more ideas on handwritten notes, including access to powerful notes others have written, visit our website: **CarriePierceNotes.com**.

Carrie Pierce is a nobody who has written absolutely nothing with the exception of this book and over 1,000 handwritten notes.

Before writing her book, Carrie got a bachelor's degree from the University of Pennsylvania in Urban Studies. After that, she ran a successful business in real estate for 20 years in Seattle, WA where she received numerous industry awards, the details of which may bore you to tears. She currently works as a Leadership Coach at Building Champions.

Carrie lives in Chalfont, PA with her three daughters and a psychotic cat named Phoebe. When she's not reading or writing you can usually find her hiding from her kids with a pint of Ben & Jerry's.

If you want to learn more about handwritten notes visit Carrie's website at: Carrie PierceNotes.com, where you can sign up to receive a newsletter with more examples and tips on handwritten notes.

www.ingramcontent.com/pod-product-compliance
Lightning Source LLC
Chambersburg PA
CBHW020400130626
46549CB00006B/2373